DIAMOND DORIS

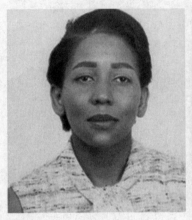

DIAMOND DORIS

The True Story of the World's
Most Notorious Jewel Thief

DORIS PAYNE

WITH ZELDA LOCKHART

AMISTAD
An Imprint of HarperCollins*Publishers*

Page ii photographs: *(left)* © Milwaukee Police Dept./Orange County Register via ZUMA Wire; *(right)* Courtesy of the author and her family

HarperCollins books may be purchased for educational, business, or sales promotional use. For information, please email the Special Markets Department at SPsales@harpercollins.com.

FIRST HARPERCOLLINS PAPERBACK EDITION PUBLISHED IN 2020

Designed by Lucy Albanese

Library of Congress Cataloging-in-Publication Data is available upon request.

ISBN 978-0-06-291800-0

20 21 22 23 24 LSC 10 9 8 7 6 5 4 3 2 1

TO BLAIR BERK,
a decent and caring woman

"You *can't* do it all. You a woman and a colored woman at that. You can't act like a man. You can't be walking around all independent-like, doing whatever you like, taking what you want, leaving what you don't."

—TONI MORRISON, *Sula*

CONTENTS

PART III: CUT

PART IV: CARAT

DIAMOND DORIS

MINED

Like people, no two diamonds are the same. They each possess characteristics that distinguish one from another. Color, Clarity, Cut, and Carat—these are the four *C*s, the characteristics that determine a diamond's value. These grading standards were established by the Gemological Institute of America (GIA) in the 1930s. But I didn't know anything about that when I was twenty-six years old. I just knew diamonds had that bling in the magazines that meant money and status. Something my family didn't have but was soon to gain.

STEPPED OUT OF THE LUKEWARM BATHWATER and felt the chill of a Cleveland spring morning. The radiator hissed to combat the cool air that seeped through the warped bathroom window. *We ain't gonna have to worry about that shit no more.* It was dusk, but like a kid waiting for Christmas morning, I had been up getting myself ready for the day that I knew was going to change things for me and Mama, and for my brother Johnny and my kids.

I went back into my bedroom no bigger than a prison cell. There was one lonely star still in the sky fighting off the rising peach color that pushed the dark blue up and away. *I've been training a long time for this day. Bring on the sun.* The radiator got to knocking. My babies—Ronny eight and Rhonda three—rolled over on their bed across from mine. I pulled the sheet up over their little brown legs. "Y'all ain't gonna want for nothing in this life if I can help it." I imagined the rooms they would each have in some big ole house when I got the whopping diamond that I saw in Mom's *Harper's Bazaar* magazine.

The linoleum on the floor was chilly to my feet but I didn't care. I had a big day ahead of me.

I sprinkled some cornstarch on my breasts, midriff, hips, and thighs, to make squeezing into my new longline bra and panty girdle easier. I slapped some on my underarms as well—I wasn't about to be hot and sweaty and perspiring today. I wrapped the opened longline bra around my torso under my breasts, with the closures in the front, sucked in, and fastened all the hooks, then twisted the bra front to back. I hunched my shoulders forward and slipped my arms through the straps, then pulled the bra up by the top and lifted it over my breasts and positioned them into the cups, pushing and adjusting until everything was in place.

Then I lay flat on my back on the bed and stepped one foot and then the other into the girdle, and wriggled it up my legs over my thighs and hips. I rolled over onto my side to stand. I yanked the girdle up and pulled the bra down to overlap, and with the help of the cornstarch, twisted and moved my body and the garments into a perfect fit.

Even after having two kids I was still slim. But now my breasts were high, my torso was long, my tummy was flat, my waist was snatched, my hips were rounded, and my thighs were trim. I had the hourglass figure I knew would get me the attention I wanted.

I sat on the edge of the bed and removed my new silk stockings from the box. I carefully gathered one stocking in my two hands to get to the base, lifted a leg, and pointed my foot. I eased the sheer hose up to my thigh and secured it with the garter snaps, then did the other leg. I stood to pull on the beige eyelet slip, stepping into satin elegance that turned me from an attendant girl at a nursing home to a Hollywood starlet preparing for her role.

I was transforming, and the linoleum now felt like a river of milk and honey beneath my feet.

My heart got to pounding in my chest as more light came into the window, casting reality on my day. *Don't chicken-shit now, Doris.* I felt excited, like it was my high school graduation day—and nervous that I was gonna fall on my face before I got my diploma. This would be the biggest ring I'd stolen, the thing to take me to the next level and get my family out of this raggedy duplex.

I laid the white blouse, green skirt, and matching suit jacket out on the bed. My nerves went away at the sight of Mom's impeccable seamstress work. This was Saks Fifth Avenue. *Yes, I'm gonna look sophisticated in this shit.* I grinned, and then quickly covered my mouth, told myself a lady smiles, she doesn't downright grin showing that she's from the West Virginia hills. This was the look I wanted— elegant, cultured, like a movie star on a spring morning.

I went over to the little nail I had hammered into the wall, reached behind to my waist, hooked the zipper on the nail, and squatted down to zip up my skirt nice and snug around my petite frame. I tucked the blouse in and eased on the jacket, smoothing the suit set into place. I sat and slipped on my new black pumps, and then did a little prance to practice the walk that I knew could turn heads. I stopped at the mirror and posed, talked politely to myself, laughed charmingly, feigned a blush, and pretended to try on a ring. It was a routine that I'd refined for acting the part of a monied woman. The most impressive part of my jewel thief costume was the wedding set.

The week before, my coworker Norma and I waltzed out of our Euclid Manor nursing home jobs on our lunch break and into the May Company department store posed as a sickly young rich white woman and her Black nurse. I walked out with a gold wedding band and a small engagement ring that I later sold at a pawnshop and used the cash to go to a different pawnshop and buy a more expensive gold wedding band with tiny inlaid diamonds and a diamond engagement ring. That new piece was a stunner—a colorless, clear two-carat ring, exquisitely cut to throw rainbows even in the pale morning light. I raised my hand up to the window, angling my finger to admire its fire. *Yes!* It was the kind of ring I saw on the fingers of the Jewish women who came to the nursing home to visit their feeble parents. The kind of ring that would make any jeweler think I was a woman of class, not a woman on a mission to steal.

The sun made its way into the sky to wake up the Black women of Hough Avenue, an alarm that said, "Tighten up your maid's uniform or nursing home uniform and get on the back of the bus to go to work." Not me. That rising sun reminded me that the jewelry stores in Pittsburgh would be opening in a couple of hours. Woo, my nerves got to going again. *Simmer down,* I told myself. I went back to the bathroom and worked on my makeup in the dim light of the single bulb that hung over the sink.

I sat on the edge of the bathtub and tore the page out of Mom's magazine. A white woman stretched her hand over a red crushed-velvet background and wore a rectangular diamond ring so big it made my mouth water. *That's the one I want.* I folded up the page, stuck it in my new purse, and took out my white gloves and clutched them in my hand. I straightened up tall, placed my new round feather-topped hat on my head, adjusted my blouse and suit, did a little turn with my purse over my forearm, and checked myself in the mirror for one last look. *You got this, Doris.*

I runway-walked through the bedroom where my children had abandoned their sleep for the smell of breakfast, then sashayed through the living room where my teenaged brother Johnny's sofa bed was a tangle of sheets, and glided into the kitchen where the audience of my family sat eating. They were unaware of what this day would bring for us, and unprepared for the sight they were about to behold.

Damn! I look better than Dorothy Dandridge!

PART I

COLOR

The highest-quality diamonds are colorless—they display an absence of color—while those of lower quality have some noticeable color. Diamond color is graded on a scale of D (colorless, a pure white) to Z (light, manifesting in a pale yellow), with the degrees of Near Colorless, Faint, and Very Light on the scale between D and Z. "Fancy-color" diamonds have greater color than a Z grade, with varying hues of yellow or brown. A D-color diamond is the highest grade and is extremely rare—the most expensive grading money can buy.

I WASN'T BORN
A JEWEL THIEF

WAS BORN RIGHT BETWEEN BIG BEAUTIFUL mountains and right between the world wars. My father was a coal miner when coal was the wealth of the nation. Black people, Native Americans, and all sorts of Europeans lived in the same town and worked together. The houses provided by the coal-mining company in Slab Fork, West Virginia, were nice. We had a four-bedroom home on Slab Fork Road, with a living and dining area, a kitchen with a pantry, and a bathroom with a tub and running water. We had two fireplaces and a kitchen stove to keep the house warm. It wasn't like the image of flies landing on your nose while you sleep that people have now when they think about mining towns.

And there was a status to the women in Slab Fork. They were stylish, and kept their kids clean, and kept fine things like embroidered doilies. They got their style from *Town & Country* and *Harper's Bazaar* magazines that arrived each month in the mail. My mom used these magazines to teach my big sister, Louise, and me how to carry yourself, how to set a table properly, how to let your household reflect international class and fine living.

Just like in any neighborhood that looks normal on the outside, things went on beneath the surface. The kids, of course, didn't understand most of it. We just looked to the grown-ups as the people in our community who sheltered and protected us, but a lot of the women slept with each other's husbands. Some women had a man and a husband, and they all knew each other and didn't mind. My daddy wasn't having none of that, though. My mother was a very attractive, refined Native American woman who had long hair down past her waist. She kept her hair braided and pinned up in two buns on either side of her head because my father didn't let her wear her hair down except in the bedroom at night.

I didn't know the word "abusive" then, but I knew my father was mean to my mother. One day, when I was about four years old, I was playing in the yard with Louise, who was keeping an eye on me. Mom used to put me on the porch swing or in the yard to play, and I could see her go all the way to Mr. Benjamin's store and come back. Mr. Benjamin was a nice Jewish man who had come to Slab Fork and built a store that was in competition with the company store. The company store never had everything a Black customer needed, but Mr. Benjamin sold pigs' feet, zoot suits, and all else in between.

That day Daddy got off the work truck and asked Louise, "Where is your mother?" She was only seven years old, but she was a big kid to me. She explained to Daddy, "Mom went to get some things from Mr. Benjamin's store. She said she'd be right back."

I quit playing with my little sticks and grass and went and sat by Louise because I could feel Daddy's mood change. He looked like a statue, watching Mom come down the road past the other houses. When she got to the gate, he went over and, with his fist like a hammer, struck her on the head. I had never seen anything like that. I got a twist in my belly. I ran at my father and beat at his pant leg. He was such a large man. I was just a scrawny little "Dink," as my father called me. He kept hitting her until she fell to the ground. I'll never forget how helpless I felt. I looked at my mom and didn't know if she was dead. It scared the shit out of me. It made me realize something: I needed to protect her. From then on, my plan was to stay by her side. I figured he wouldn't hit her with his little Dink in the way.

OF MY FOUR siblings, my brother Albert was the oldest; then my sister, Louise; my brother Clarence; and David Junior; and then came me. We were what they called stair-step children, with just enough space between our ages for Mom to recover from childbirth. For seven years, I had Mom all to myself. Then my brother Johnny came along.

A lot of shit displeased me when he came into the picture, getting all of my mother's attention. He'd cry and she'd pick him up, and I didn't like it one bit. My mom would buy applesauce and tell me I could feed him. I guess she was trying to make me feel special, but when she would whisper to her friends about me being jealous, I would eat the whole bowl of applesauce. After Johnny was born, I didn't ease off being by my mother's side. He was just a baby—what was he going to do to keep Mom safe? Instead, I grew even more fiercely protective of her.

When I was about eight years old, Johnny would take his nap, and those were good times when I had Mom all to myself. I would stand on a chair and be right by her side and blow my breath on the kitchen window to watch it fog up, and use my finger to draw pictures while she took care of whatever kitchen chores she had.

One day in late October I was in the kitchen with Mom. I was standing on the chair and peering out the window. I looked out over her garden and the shed, which was my playhouse in the spring and summer, but it was about to become a shed again filled with wood for winter. I saw that Mrs. Dickson's cow had gotten into our garden where the tomatoes were. They were some of the only things still growing.

I had heard "the cow jumped over the moon" story, so I eased out from my mother's side and took the broken string from my drawstring panties. The plan was to get the pin out of my panties and to catch the cow's tail as she whipped it past the warped door of the shed. I wasn't going to let her eat my mother's tomatoes, so I was going to send her to jump over the moon.

There I was, holding my knees to keep my drawers up, and the cow's tail was whipping back and forth. I got the pin out of my mouth and held her tail and stuck the pin in it. The cow kicked the door and I don't remember anything else. She had kicked me onto the door and the door right off the hinges. When I came to, I got up and ran into the house crying, "Mom, the cow threw me over the moon."

Mom had been watching out the window, I guess wondering what I was up to, and when I ran into the kitchen, she was on the floor shaking with laughter. She said, "What on earth is wrong with you?" She told me that when she saw that cow kick, she couldn't tell if I was glued to the door or if I was riding it. She couldn't handle herself laughing.

In my scheming to take out that cow, that cow fucked me up. I had cow shit on me, my drawers were down by my ankles, my dress was up in the air, and I had skin off my elbows with grass cuts. Little Johnny was still asleep in his crib. I didn't think it was funny at all; I wanted her to see that the cow was about to eat her tomatoes, and that I could protect her.

It wasn't an everyday thing that my father beat my mother, but she was a prisoner. He didn't want her talking to any men and didn't even want her talking or gossiping with women. This taught me early in life that abusers try to isolate you. Those days, I would go to the shed near my mom's garden, where in the spring and summer poke salad greens grew wild beside the tomatoes and cucumbers.

I had an electric iron and other little fake kitchen things, including a fake husband I called Vernon. I came up with that idea because in our school play I had been cast as the wife of my classmate Vernon Burks. I had such a good imagination, I really thought Vernon was mine. After the play, nobody told me different.

Out in my playhouse, I beat on Vernon the way I thought my mother should beat back my father. I had a pile of rocks for whenever I saw my imaginary husband not acting right. My mom gave me leftover food from the kitchen so I could play my little husband-and-wife game, and if Vernon ate anything before I told him he could, I knocked the shit out of him. If I was cooking and he came talking some mess to me, I threw the hot food on him. I felt satisfied, like I was really doing something to discipline my father. I now understood how even if men might make good protectors, you couldn't let them think for one minute that they were in control of your house. When my mom passed by the playhouse and heard me screaming and beating on Vernon, she said, "God, don't tell me I gave birth to the devil."

I knew from that early age that I was going to have to protect my mom. And that no man was going to make me a prisoner in my own home, or abuse me, or beat me—and if a man ever thought of striking me, that was going to be the end of him.

CHAPTER 2

GREED

WEST VIRGINIA USED TO HAVE THE BEST schools in the nation. If your kid wasn't in school, you were charged three dollars for each day your child was out. But with Black and white families streaming in from the South to take advantage of the demand for more men to dig all of that coal out of the mountain, the enforcement of education fell to the wayside.

Shacks were built down near the coal-mine mountain to accommodate the newcomers. They weren't built as well as our home. There was this one family—I don't know how many kids they had, but they had a bunch. They were all dark-haired white children who looked alike. The one girl my age just looked sad to me, never at school, always looking like she hadn't eaten. That was the time when West Virginia coal-mining towns started to get their reputation as slums. The greedy mining companies made a ton of money off folks groveling for jobs that promised a better life, but the companies didn't spend a dime of their riches on nicer housing or safer mines.

One fall morning I sat in my sixth-grade classroom barely paying attention. Out the window, the leaves were orange, red, and yellow against the blue skies. Those were the most beautiful mornings, and my favorite time of year in the mountains.

My teacher, Mrs. MacArthur, was a tall, thin white woman who wore her blond-and-silver hair in a bun. She kept a Bible on her desk right next to our math, history, and literature books. There was a Baptist church in our town, but we didn't ever go. Mom just stuck to reciting the Catholic Mass from her upbringing and telling me I better be good so Baby Jesus wouldn't be mad. That was the extent of my biblical knowledge.

Mrs. MacArthur's stern voice and West Virginia accent could cut you in two. "Doris Payne, eyes up here." The lesson for our world history that day was greed. She stood up there in her gray straight-up-and-down dress. It was tight, buttoned to her neck. She wore no lipstick, had no sense of fashion, and loved to quote the Bible in her piercing accent. "Luke 12:15. 'Take heed, and beware of covetousness: for a man's life consisteth not in the abundance of the things which he possesseth.'"

I propped up my chin with my hand. *You can say that because you don't possesseth anything.*

After lunch, Mrs. MacArthur discussed mining since that's what our neck of the woods was all about. She presented several different kinds of mining—mining for coal, mining for oil, mining for gold, and mining for diamonds.

She went on gesturing and teaching and preaching. "The slaves did all the mining for the pharaohs."

She went over to the pastel-colored map and pointed out the places in Africa where diamonds were being mined. "Toil not to be rich, children." She drove her fist down like she was driving a fence post. "Plant only the fruits thy need for thy family's sake"—then she pulled her fist up—"And pluck only from the earth for thy family's sake."

The entire class fidgeted with their notebooks, just waiting for the bell to ring. My friend Lil kept her hand over her mouth the way I did, trying not to laugh. "Luke 12:21: 'So is he that layeth up treasure for himself and is not rich toward God.'"

I pulled my hand from my mouth and raised it above my head, my fingers wriggling.

Mrs. MacArthur let out a weighted sigh before calling on me. "Doris."

"Does the Raleigh Company layeth up riches of coal, and everybody daddy is the slave for getting the coal?" The class broke out in roaring laughter. She sent me home with a note for my mom. I gave it to Daddy since he couldn't read.

The next morning Daddy got on the work truck with his lunch pail. He wore his hard hat with a lamp that was so smudged with black I didn't know what color it really was.

The truck headed to the Beckley mine ten miles up the road. That day Mrs. MacArthur paused in the middle of the lesson. We didn't know what she was listening for until we realized she was listening to the air siren, which had churned up from a low whistle to a full blasting scream. The siren was cranked only when there was an accident in any of the Raleigh Company mines. I felt a knot in my gut.

The siren quieted, and Mrs. MacArthur went on with the lesson. She glanced periodically at the window and the classroom door. If there was no commotion outside, then it wasn't the Slab Fork mine, but Daddy and most of the men were at Beckley that day.

All six of us Payne children walked home with the Lester brothers, our neighbors, whose family had eight boys. We went into Mr. Benjamin's store, and he waved us back out. "You all want to get on home. There was an accident at Beckley."

Mom had left a note at our house: "Augustus got hurt. He's okay. I will be in Beckley."

LOUISE SAT AT the table the next morning and read us the newspaper. "The blast killed two: Jackson Lester, forty-two, of Slab Fork, and Mason Bond, forty, of Slab Fork. Five others were injured. Senator-elect M. M. Neely says yesterday's accident is further reason to push the measure through the House of Representatives for safety inspections of West Virginia mines."

Daddy's right leg and foot had gotten caught in the slate that fell that day. I hated what he was doing to my mother, but he did make sure we had everything we asked for. We had school shoes, Sunday shoes, a washer with a good wringer on it, and nice sheets. The Lester boys' father had been killed by the accident. I felt guilty sitting there with Louise and my brothers. I had fantasies of hurting Daddy to make him leave Mom alone. I wanted Daddy punished, but I didn't want him crushed under a pile of rubble like some slave who built temples for pharaohs.

DURING MY FATHER'S recovery, we packed up and the whole family got the bus to Mount Airy, North Carolina, to stay at our grandmother's house. She lived in the country with a lot of space between her house and Aunt Reece's place. There were chickens and pigs, old craggy winter trees to climb. And Daddy's mood was softer. He received a settlement for his injuries while he recovered, which he generously shared in gifts and groceries with his mother and his sister. He would come into the kitchen, where Mom and Grandma were making breakfast, and actually say "Good morning." I felt like that was the happiest I ever saw him.

ON THE NIGHT of December 7, 1941, I was the only person at Grandma's house. Everybody else had gone up the road to Aunt Reece's house for dinner. They had been whispering all day. I figured about something they thought I was too young to know about, like money or what Mom called "grown-folk's business." My mother had told me, "Get your coat on, Dink." I didn't care about any of their grown talk. I had told her to go on without me. I wanted to be by myself and listen to the radio.

Glenn Miller's "Chattanooga Choo Choo" was playing. I threw my skinny self all over the room, dancing like I had a partner. Then the news came on and I heard what all the whispering had been about. A man came on: "President Roosevelt said in a statement today that the Japanese have attacked Pearl Harbor, Hawaii, from the air."

Chills went through my body, from the top of my head to my knees. I remembered Daddy and our neighbor Mr. Withers saying the Japanese were coming and were going to take over the world. I ran to the door and searched up and down the road to see if tanks were coming with their lights blaring. All I saw were the lights at Aunt Reece's house. Nighttime in Slab Fork was only this dark if you walked yourself right out of the town. House lights and lights from the mine and the businesses at each end of the road kept things lit up. Out in Mount Airy, there was a deep darkness that made you feel like you were swimming in blue ink. It was so dark I had to stand still for a minute. I tilted my head up to the sky to see if there were planes about to drop bombs. There were just cold stars. I thought it must be too dark to see the bombs. I didn't put my coat on. I ran to Aunt

Reece's house, scared to death, screaming, "The Japanese are coming!" I thought that might be my last day on Earth. Of course, everybody had the news already except me.

After a few weeks, Daddy was mending nicely, and he was needed back at the mines. Mom said, "Soon as we have New Year's dinner, we're headed home."

I got that knot in my tummy again. I hollered, "I'm not going anywhere. Mom and I are staying here." Everybody laughed, thinking I was still scared of the Japanese, but I didn't want to go back to the way things had been in our house.

When we got home, the boys teased me when they saw me clinging to Mom. They stood in front of her. "You can't go near her, Girly."

I tried to dodge around them until I got good and mad and laid into Albert with a fury of punches that just made him laugh.

Albert turned eighteen that January and got called to serve in the military. He was sent to Patterson Air Force Base in Dayton, Ohio. Shortly after, Clarence got called up to Raleigh County, West Virginia. By the time I was fourteen, my brother David, who was only sixteen, went off to the Navy. Mom was broken. The boys had never even slept a night away from home. She sat at the table crying, shaking her head. "Fighting for a country that has no respect for us."

My brothers wrote me letters from France, England, and Switzerland, and I read them over and over. I took them to school with me and stood in front of the map. I figured out all the places where they were. I imagined Albert sitting in a British pub speaking in an English accent with white British soldiers. Mrs. MacArthur let me clip out the newspaper articles describing all the places in the world where battles were being waged. I did my geography reports on the history and society of those countries. I learned my geography well I suppose, but I did not yet know that I would one day be in those places, stealing some of the most precious diamonds imaginable.

CHAPTER 3

MY DECLARATION
OF WAR

EVERYTHING IN SLAB FORK FELT DEPRESSING.
Some houses that had ten or eleven kids were almost
empty. Their sons and the younger husbands had been
sent off to serve in the military. Things in our own house
were depressing and so much worse for Mom without the
boys there.

One day in the summer of 1942 the younger Lester brothers who hadn't had to go off to war came down and played
cards with me and Louise and Mom. We kept the back door
open to catch a breeze. The iceman had stopped coming
to the neighborhood, but we drank water and pretended it
had ice in it. To place our bets, we used for money what
we had in abundance: pinto beans, which grew so plentiful
the vines crawled up the sides of people's houses. We got to
whooping and hollering, laughing at each other and having

a good ole time. Bernard Lester didn't want to play cards with us. He just wanted to brush Mom's long hair. I thought that was sweet but also thought, *Don't let my daddy catch you doing that.* Nobody thought Bernard liked women in that way, but that wouldn't matter to my father.

I heard the roaring motor and squeaking brakes of the work truck. It roared, then squeaked to drop a man off, then roared and squeaked. Mom said, "Louise, what time is it?"

Dad didn't usually come home until five o'clock or later. "It ain't but three o'clock, Mom."

Daddy's boot steps sounded on the porch. There must have been an accident in one of the mines, and they had closed to respect the dead. Mom got serious and was trying to pull her hair together, but me and Louise were still acting silly. We got to teasing Bernard. "Ooo! Our daddy's gonna see you got his woman. Boy, you better run."

Bernard and his brothers went tearing out the back door like they were about to get a serious beatdown. Louise and I were doubled over laughing when Daddy came into the kitchen. He took one look at Mom and dropped his lunch pail on the floor. We got silent. He yelled at Mom, "Go to bed right now!" It was three o'clock in the afternoon, but Mom gathered up her stuff and shuffled to the bedroom like she was some little kid who had done wrong. Louise and I looked at each other. We were fed up with seeing her treated that way. Daddy followed behind Mom and slammed the bedroom door. We didn't know what went on behind those doors that night, but I knew it was bad for Mom.

The next day was a Saturday, and Mom tried to make like things were regular. She had a big knot on her cheekbone. I kept imagining different things that he might have hit her with: his fist, the baseball bat he kept leaned against the wall.

Daddy stayed in bed. Me, Louise, and Mom had breakfast and didn't speak about it. I didn't see any other visible bruises, but then again, Mom was wearing a long-sleeved cotton dress in the summer heat.

I did the dishes and sat in the kitchen with the back door open. Thank goodness it was raining, which made the heat bearable. Mom put on a pot of pinto beans and said without looking at me, "Dink, watch the beans."

I worked on cutting out fashion photos from *Town & Country* magazines to make paper dolls. Louise was in our room hogging the record player, which was supposed to be for both of us. She listened to the records Mom told her not to buy down at Mr. Benjamin's store: "Hard Driving Mama" and "Salty Papa Blues." Mom said those were about things I had no business hearing, so Louise always hunkered down on the bedroom floor and listened on Saturdays. David was home on leave and was still asleep in the boys' room.

I heard Daddy's big feet stomping across the floor, and then I heard a thud like a whole body falling to the floor. I got up and saw him in the living room in his work pants but no shirt on. Mom was on the floor, already curled up, and he went over and kicked her in the ribs. The sound she made when the air left her body made me go rigid with fear, and then he fell down on his knees to punch her. The baseball bat was too far away.

I turned back to the stove, grabbed the pot of beans, and walked the pot real steady into the living room. "Get off her! Get off my mom!" I yelled, but he didn't. I stood over him with the pot like he was Vernon in my playhouse, and I poured.

I got his attention real good. I got David's attention too. He ran into the living room and put his arms around Daddy's wide body like he was rescuing one of his buddies in some combat training. He and Daddy hobbled to the bathtub, and David poured cups of cold water over Daddy's burned back. I didn't care anything about what my daddy was needing right then. I had needed him to get off my mom, so I had done what I had trained myself to do with Vernon.

I didn't run. I stood there, with the pot in my hand. My mom got up and yelled, "Go put the pot down, Dink," like I was going to burn her too. She had that look in her eyes like when I was practicing on Vernon and she would pray that she hadn't given birth to a bad seed.

I didn't say anything to her. I just waited to see if Daddy was coming back. Louise stood in the door of our bedroom with her hand over her mouth. That bad song was playing behind her, which just made me madder.

I said papa why you so salty
Why do you bring me down?
There's no complaint
When my other man comes around

My sister could listen to bad music, but she couldn't do anything to protect Mom.

When Daddy came out of the bathroom with the wet towel on his back, he just looked at me and said, "I'll be damned." He never punished me for what I did. I think somewhere inside his concern for his own mother, he understood that I was the one in the house who felt like I had to take care of things for my mom.

LOUISE AND I sat my mom down. "Leave him!" we said, knowing it might mean not being by her side. I had never been away from her.

A few days later, Mom left. She first hid out at Daddy's mother's house in North Carolina. Louise went to see her a couple of times, but I didn't know anything about how to do that. Then Mom talked with a family friend who lived in our town, Mrs. Scott. Mom didn't have a high school diploma, but as a young girl she had worked at a Catholic monastery in Minnesota where her own mother was a cook. There she had learned to sew, and her mother had passed down a respect for refined behavior and manners and etiquette. She also got a basic education and learned Catholic religious traditions at the monastery. Mrs. Scott had a daughter, Leona, who helped Mom get a job as an alteration seamstress at Saks Fifth Avenue in New York City.

That first couple of weeks after Mom left, I cried myself to sleep. Part of me wondered why she hadn't asked me to go with her. Didn't she realize everything I had been doing to keep her safe? After a few nights, I finished all that crying shit and just missed her.

Mom sent me clippings of their finest dresses. My heart hurt that I couldn't be in New York. I taped the clippings to my and Louise's bedroom wall along with my paper doll fashions clipped out of *Harper's Bazaar, Vogue,* and the other fashion magazines that still came in the mail even though there was no longer the ritual of walking to the company store with Mom to get the mail and walking back up Slab Fork Road with her, the magazines in one arm, as her elegant gait quickened so we could sit at the table and flip the pages. Mom wasn't there to read them, but I kept the custom of clipping the fashions.

Louise and I walked with Johnny to school every day. Dad went to work and came home and never said a word to us about Mom. It wasn't awful. At least without her there to beat on, he didn't beat on anybody else. It wasn't good either. It was just empty.

SHE HADN'T BEEN gone quite a year, and one day I got my period. I didn't know what to do. I had tried to solve the mystery of sanitary pads when I was eight or nine with no success. Back then, I had found a box of sanitaries under the tub. I had never seen them before, and they had been hidden, so I thought, *This must be something to know about.*

I put a few on the gate out in front of the house. I figured my daddy would get off the work truck and tell me what they were.

He looked at those on the gate and then at my little eight-year-old self and said, "I'll be damned." He called my mom. "Clima! You have to see this."

When I got my period, Louise, who was sixteen years old, told me what to do with the sanitaries. But I didn't want her. I told her, "I don't want you looking at me. I want Mom."

She used to work so hard to be the grown-up. "Mom's not here. Now quit acting a fool."

My gut hurt all the time. *Why would God do this to women?* I wanted to die, the pain was so bad.

Louise walked me up to Mr. Benjamin's store for some pain powders, and I stood outside. I refused to go in and let people in the community know what was happening to me. I wouldn't go to school because I didn't want my classmates to know what was happening to me either. Louise couldn't handle me anymore. Somehow she got a message to our mother. I think she told Leona's mother, Mrs. Scott, and Mom sent word that she would come back. I was going to be happy again.

AFTER MOM RETURNED, there was a difference in the atmosphere in the house for a while, until Daddy started getting jealous. "How many times a day do you have to go to that store? Who's up there you going to see?" Mom only went to the store once a day. She probably enjoyed talking to Mr. Benjamin. I sure did. It was a highlight for me to go to the store and tell him what I had been reading about or studying, and he always listened. He told me I was a smart kid. Mom said he was so nice to us because as a Jewish man he knew what it was like to be mistreated. Since the iceman had stopped coming, we couldn't keep food cool. What was she supposed to do except go to the store every day?

She went back to not having a life again. This was the difference between me and my mom. I was never going to have a man control me in my own house. I would always make my own money, and I was going to have to take care of me and mine. But at that point I didn't know how I was going to do that.

CHAPTER 4

MR. BENJAMIN

UNTIL MOM'S SEAMSTRESS MONEY RAN OUT, she was a good provider for us rather than relying just on Daddy. Every two weeks she gave me and Louise money to go get our hair pressed. It was a ritual that made us feel good about our looks. The beautician, Mrs. Jackson, would pay to use the kitchen space in one of the neighbors' houses in the community and do everybody's hair.

One day, when it was time for Mrs. Jackson to come to town, Mom gave me five dollars—three dollars for my hair and two dollars for me to put on the grocery account in Mr. Benjamin's store. Mom told me, "Dink, you been working so hard in history and geography in school. If you get any of that reward money for good grades, I'm going to buy you a watch." In my eighth-grade class, prize money was given for being good in school. Mom said, "While you're in the store, take a look and see which watch you might want." Off I went to get my hair done and pay on the grocery bill.

I sat for hours waiting. I didn't mind one bit because I spent the time looking through magazines. I studied the straight, beautiful hair of the white women who had been photographed looking like they were dashing away from some ball. I told Mrs. Jackson, "That's what I want," and she said, pulling the magazine away to see it better, "Baby, don't you know I cain't get it that straight?"

I didn't feel any less than any of the young women in the magazines. Style was style, and made for allure, and magnetism, and envy, and I loved fashion, beautiful hairdos, and a look of class. How was I supposed to know as a child that the world imposed a difference between some women and others?

I remember one hot day, when I was nine years old, hearing Mom and the older kids talk about Rhett Butler and Scarlett O'Hara in *Gone with the Wind*. It seemed like everywhere I went in our neighborhood people were talking about these two characters like they were something special everybody ought to know about.

The movie didn't play till that night, but the doors were already open on the first night so the reels could be brought in and the theater could be cleaned. Albert and Clarence were on the cleaning crew. They got to be there when the folks brought in the reels and tested them out. I walked my little self right in there like I had some business to take care of. Nobody paid me any attention. I scrunched myself down in one of the comfortable seats and watched the movie, trying to figure out what all the fuss was about. There was a lot of adult talk, and I didn't know what I was listening to, except how pretty Scarlett was and how pretty her clothes, the houses, the great lawns were. Then there was that Black woman telling her to take a nap, and it wasn't long before I started to get sleepy. The last thing I remembered was Scarlett lying in bed.

Then some lady who was sweeping the theater woke me up and told me to run along home. I just kept thinking about how beautiful Scarlett O'Hara's fine dresses were, her teardrop jewels, her hair all pressed and curled, and those white pillows all around her.

My brothers laughed when I came to the table that night. I had a pocketbook my mom had given me to act out my Miss Lady game in my playhouse. I tried to speak proper like Scarlett O'Hara, and they laughed at me even harder. I had put white cornstarch all over my face as my makeup, and my red lipstick was everywhere except on my lips.

"Fiddledeedee. War, war, war."

David reared back and smacked the table. "Girly. You ain't gonna grow up to be Scarlett. You gonna grow up to be Mammy."

I remembered that big woman sticking her head out the window, calling after Scarlett, and I said something awful. "I'm not Black like Mammy."

I went to hit David with my big purse, and the others cracked up at my whiteface.

Albert said, "Mom, you ought to stop her from doing that. You ought to stop that girl."

I said, "I am not a girl. I'm a goil," talking in my new accent.

I THOUGHT MRS. JACKSON did a good job. My press and curl was stiff, but I looked pretty cute.

When I walked in the store that day, I didn't see Mr. Benjamin, but his niece stood behind the glass counter, counting change. She was a dark-haired, pale-skinned young woman around Louise's age who didn't smile much. She scratched her calculations in a ledger and said, "Doris, your mom's bill is two dollars." I gave her the money Mom owed on her account. She didn't even look up and smile. Just took the money and kept doing her numbers.

I asked her, "Mr. Benjamin here?" I was anxious to tell him my news about Mom agreeing to buy me a watch. Mr. Benjamin would ask me how my family was doing or how I was doing in school. I never said Daddy beat Mom or that she once had run away from home. Mom had taught me better than to run my mouth out in the streets about family business.

I was glad when Mr. Benjamin came out of the back room. He was a thick, olive-skinned man with black hair who wore a white dress shirt and a tie even under his apron. I thought that was a weird choice of uniform when he was sometimes cutting and wrapping meat for the icebox and other times rolling bolts of fabric.

"How are you doing today, Miss Doris?" He reached into a jar of gumdrops and gave me one. He always talked like his nose was stopped up. "That's on the house," he said. My daddy would have whipped my butt if he saw me take something free from that man.

I thanked him and told him my news while chewing on the gummy treat. "Mom said she is going to buy me a watch. All I have to do is get good grades and the top prize. I already get good grades, and I might be the smartest girl at my school." I was still jabbering on, but he had heard "Mom is going to buy me a watch."

"That's a coincidence. I got some fine watches in just the other day." He shooed his niece away from behind the counter. She frowned and disappeared up the stairs to where they lived. He bent all the way over to use the key around his neck to open the glass case. "Take a look and tell me which one of these you think you're going to be wanting when you win that prize money." He had as much confidence in me as I did, and I liked that. He leaned on the glass with one elbow. I thought his weight might collapse the thing.

"Here." He put a few of the watches on my arm. "What do you think, Doris? Those look really fine, don't they?" He smiled the way he always did, never showing his teeth, as if he was embarrassed by them. I liked that he talked to me the same way he did with the grown-ups. He respected that I was a smart young woman.

Then something happened. A white fellow with a big booming voice and overalls came into Mr. Benjamin's store. "Hey, Bill!" And Mr. Benjamin immediately switched up on me with his demeanor. He snatched the watches off my arm. He shoved them back into the case, leaned over, locked it, and took off his apron all in one quick move. He shot me a mean look with his face more angled at this man than at me. He looked at me like somebody he didn't like or didn't want in his way. Then he shook that big redneck man's hand, and the two of them slapped each other on the shoulder.

It bothered me like a nightmare or stories Daddy used to tell about men getting crushed in the mine. I felt a hurt in the middle of my chest.

In his rush to serve the redneck, he forgot how many watches he had put on my arm. I was still wearing one. This white man had seen him treating a little Black girl like a human being, and Mr. Benjamin didn't want to fall out of his favor, so he was now going to a lot of trouble to change things up. He told me in a mean tone, "Run along, little girl." I had never seen his face like that, like he was mimicking the rednecks, who looked at me mean if I walked too close to them. I didn't think of Mr. Benjamin as white, but that moment changed everything.

White men would be in town in the street shooting craps, and I would stand over their shoulder trying to figure it all out. They would get that scowl on their faces and say, "Run along," and shoo me away. Daddy would be waiting for Louise to read him the paper on those days when my mom left us alone. I would grab it and try to read to Daddy about the war. Daddy would yank it out of my hand and say, "Run along, Dink," not recognizing that I could take care of myself, take care to keep him from beating Mom if I wanted to.

I looked down at the watch that was still on my arm. *I'll show Mr. Benjamin not to go treating me like that.* I went all the way over to the door, acting like I was leaving. Then I looked at my arm, pretending to notice the watch there for the first time, and I hollered, "Oh, Mr. Benjamin. You forgot this one." That redneck heard it too and looked wide-eyed at Mr. Benjamin. He was surprised that Mr. Benjamin trusted and liked me enough to let me try on watches in his store. I could see that whatever had afflicted Mr. Benjamin and made him switch up on me fell on him with the white man's stare. That's how I wanted it.

He stammered and stuttered, and I took it off nice and slow and put it in his hand without touching him. The two of them stared at me like some strange thing that had interrupted their conversation. I went out the door, opening it hard so the bell above the door would ring and letting it slam so it would make even more noise. I walked back home, passing that damned mountain of coal, and stomped into the house.

I was so mad that I tore off the wall all of my paper dolls of fine white ladies in fine expensive clothes and jewels. I felt demeaned. It was the worst feeling I ever had, even today.

I took the *Harper's Bazaar* magazine and cut the hell out of the women in it. Those models with their pillbox hats, tapered suits, and diamond bracelets weren't better than me. Mr. Benjamin standing there like a king with his jewels locked up wasn't better than me either.

I was ready for war against him and all of his brothers.

PART II

CLARITY

A diamond's clarity is graded on its absence of internal flaws, or inclusions, and its lack of external characteristics, or blemishes. The clarity scale consists of six grades, with some subcategories with subgrades: Flawless (F or FL); Internally Flawless (IF); Very, Very Slightly Included (with two subgrades, VVS1 and VVS2); Very Slightly Included (also with two subgrades, VS1 and VS2); Slightly Included (also with two subgrades, SI1 and SI2); and Included (with three subgrades, I1, I2, and I3). The clarity of the diamond affects its appearance and its value. The higher up the scale closer to Flawless, the more expensive the diamond. A perfectly flawless diamond is so rare that most jewelers and gemologists will never see one in their lifetime.

CHAPTER 5

TRICKSTER IN PRACTICE

ONE SPRING MORNING, LIL AND I STOOD OUT-side her family's little shack. The musty odor from days of rain breezed out the open door. The sun beat down on the two of us so hard it threatened to undo our press and curls. We looked fine and ladylike—me in my white-collared, chiffon-yellow cotton church dress and my white church gloves, and Lil in her blue-and-white gingham dress and white gloves. We were sixteen but could easily have passed for grown women.

Mrs. Jackson had promised to give us a ride to her town of Bridgeport. She had a cream-colored DeSoto with white-walls that she could afford after all of her years of doing hair. After that short ride, we would take a three-hour bus trip to Cleveland, where we would spend the rest of the day and return on the bus. We planned to get a ride home from

Bridgeport with Mr. Withers, who had to pick up his fur-loughed son at the bus station. It took a hell of a lot of figur-ing, but we wouldn't be bored that weekend. We'd be grown and free.

Lil fidgeted nonstop with the hem of her dress. I smacked at her hand and told her, "Girl, you can't be acting all ner-vous. That will draw way too much attention." I straight-ened her collar. "We just going to Cleveland to have fun."

I told her what I had done in Mr. Benjamin's store. "I can make people forget that I'm wearing their jewelry and make them know it's all their fault. I can make it happen anywhere. Even the department stores."

She made the mistake of doubting me. "Doris, you crazy. A white man will put you in jail faster than you can say 'Boo.'"

I had to prove to her that by the time anyone heard me say "Boo," I would be long gone with the jewels.

On the bus, we pulled the windows down and let the sun and wind blow through our loose curls. The world went from the snug, narrow roads of West Virginia to wide-open spaces where cars and buses and people were a constant stream. Folks on the bus kept glancing at us, and that just made us giggle. We giggled so much we didn't even think about or have enough sense to know all the trouble we could get ourselves into.

In Cleveland, we hopped on the back of a trolley and got off at the next stop without paying the fare.

We strolled up Euclid Avenue. I told Lil, "Get it together. No more giggling." I said to her, "Look. Walk like this."

I led out in front with my head up, like Scarlett O'Hara. "Keep your head up, Lil, and when we pause to look in a window, hold one of your hands in the other like this."

She did as instructed and said, "I'm gonna look like I own the place." We got to giggling again before we straightened up.

We stood outside the Woolworth's, and I told Lil, "Look, when we get in there, just go sit down at the malt counter. But keep an eye on me and how I'm about to make this man forget." I walked away from her. When I looked back, I could see her leg bouncing with nerves.

The man behind the jewelry counter looked like J. Edgar Hoover. He asked me if I'd like to see the watches in the case. "Yes, please."

I tried one on, told him some lie about my father selling land his family owned in West Virginia and our family recently moving to Cleveland. I let him believe I was as old as a college girl.

"Are you a college student?"

I didn't miss a beat and told him another lie. "Yes, I'm a freshman at University of Akron. I'm home for the weekend." We got into a big conversation about the impact of the war on the world's economy. He was so impressed with me and what I knew. He would have shit his pants if he knew my father couldn't read and was at home lying in the bed, waiting for something right to happen in life. I knew that displaying my intelligence along with my fine way of dressing was key.

He relaxed and fell into a comfortable conversation.

"You are such a nice young lady," he said twice. Then he saw me off.

I got to the malt counter. I showed Lil the watch under my glove, and she spat the malt back into her glass. The two of us almost bust out laughing, but I nudged her to be quiet.

I turned and went back to the jewelry counter. "Pardon me, sir. You forgot to take this watch back. Hold on to it, though. My daddy will be coming back to buy it." I turned on one heel with my purse over my forearm, one elbow bent, the other swinging by my side, as I switched over to the counter like a model and hooked arm in arm with Lil.

"Thank you, young lady!" he called behind me.

Lil and I walked calmly out of the store. When we got to the street, we ran and laughed like two cackling witches who had stolen the heart out of the chest of the king's first-born son. We were as high as we could be. We were secretly in control of white men.

"Told you I could do it. I told you."

"You sure did."

THAT WAS OUR weekend fun for many Saturdays to come. With each time, I gained confidence until it wasn't a challenge anymore. What I knew from my adventures with Lil and from that day in Mr. Benjamin's store was that I could make people forget. If they could forget, then I could get money. Of course there was risk in taking on this lifestyle.

I had never met anyone who had been to jail, but I knew I didn't want to end up there.

I stopped riding into Cleveland to show off with Lil. I spent all of my time figuring out how I was going to groom myself to take jewels.

I knew I had to look the part of somebody who had everything in life she wanted and didn't need to steal anything. I spent more time clipping souvenir outfits out of Mom's magazines. I clipped out jewelry, shoes, and purses. I noticed the respect the folks got who walked into Woolworth's wearing the right price tag and with their mountain twang smoothed out. When that happened, the store clerks didn't care who they were, just looked at their shoes, their jewelry, and perked up, and if a customer looked and sounded like they were from the hills, they got served in due time. When Louise wasn't in the room, I practiced my British accent. Louise looked up at the wall one day and said, "Girly, you too big for playing Miss Lady. Take that taped-up shit down off the wall."

I gave her that look she and Mom used to say was my devilish look. "Ain't nobody playing Miss Lady." I rolled back over on my bed to cut some fine jewels out of a magazine. I knew what I was doing. There wasn't nothing about it that was play. It was practice. I knew if I could perfect a plan, I could make good money.

CHAPTER 6

FINDING MY WAY OUT

ATER THAT YEAR, THE COAL MINES BEGAN TO falter. Accidents were a regular occurrence. There were strikes to improve working conditions for miners. Some strikes were successful, under the leadership of union president John L. Lewis, but some just resulted in lean times because there was less demand for coal.

My father, like most of the men, resigned himself to waiting for things to get better. Every Friday, Daddy stayed in bed snoring all day. Mom and the other wives and their older girl children piled onto the bus and went to the Raleigh Company in Beckley to pick up their husbands' little severance checks, which didn't cover all the bills. The parking lot of the Raleigh Company also held Harper's Market, an open-air farmers' market that sold vegetables, bread, eggs, butchered meat, and even livestock. Mom made whatever she could with things from our garden, but it was fall, and she could only make so many meals with greens, onions, and tomatoes. I needed to do something to get us some food.

At the market, I observed the way the whole thing went with the women in line for food at the stalls. One held the place in line while one of them dashed over to the other line to get her husband's severance paycheck. I noticed the confusion that happened for the farmers at their stalls once a woman got up to the market counter and bagged up food only to say that it was for a friend who was in the other line and coming back to sign over her check for the food. I watched the farmer's wife or kids get confused between whom they were holding which bags for, and how much people owed. I walked from stall to stall watching this.

Confusion was opportunity.

I went to the longest market line with Mom's list. I heard the two clerks, red-headed farm girls my age, arguing because the one working the line was ready to take a break. I filled a bag with potatoes, weighed it, and set it aside; filled one with carrots and set it aside; one with a bunch of greens and set it aside. "Can you hurry up?" the one farm girl said in her West Virginia drawl.

"Okay," I said back in a country drawl just like hers.

"All right," she said in a more understanding tone once she had heard my familiar, but fake, drawl. I hadn't planned to do that, but it seemed like a good thing to make her trust me.

I drawled again, "I'm gonna set this over here for my

mom, who's in the payment line." I took one bag, fiddled around with some beets that I had decided not to get, but then stuck those in the bags too. I was making a confusing, fiddling mess for the farm girl, and the people in line were getting agitated and making her want her break even more.

After a while that red-headed girl was so exasperated, she yelled out to her sister, "Carolyn, I'm going on break!"

She put the OUT TO LUNCH sign up on the counter, and everybody in line grumbled and went to another stall. I just grabbed the bags of produce, swiped the three dollars somebody else left on the counter for their payment, and went over to Mom in the other line with my arms full. I put my head on her shoulder while we stepped up in line. Once she signed for the check, I said, "I got a surprise for you." We went out to the muddy parking lot. We didn't wait for the bus. I went over to where the cabs were. I handed the fellow two dollars and said like a proper lady, "Slab Fork, please." With my mom half smiling and half glaring at me, off we went with the groceries, and still we had a dollar left over.

That day I was just doing what was necessary to get us enough food. But I had uncovered the keys to getting away with stealing jewels: confusion and familiarity.

DURING THOSE YEARS, I helped out using my new talent. I think Mom was suspicious because she never questioned me. I told her, "Here, I found some money on the side of the road." She would give me that through-the-shed-slats look and life would go on, with us having what we needed.

One of my side jobs was at school. I knew this girl named Deedee. She and I were friends because I stole and gave her things and she stole and gave me things. We had each other's backs, and in my day that meant more than anything. That year the principal sold candy to raise money, and Deedee stole the whole money box with the candy in it. The two of us split it. Here's a lesson you can take from Doris: I never let anybody other than the person I was partnered with know I ever did that or anything wrong. I knew how to cover my tracks so there was no way of finding out what I had done. To this day, any confessing I was going to do would be in order to make things better for myself.

Mom eventually got a seamstress job at a department store in Cleveland, and we planned to move there with my little brother, Johnny. We were leaving Daddy for good, and the money from selling the candy would be a big help.

"Where you get that from, Dink?" Mom asked.

"I helped the principal sell candy. She gave me and Deedee some of the profits." A lie close to the truth was a good lie. It wasn't until I was a grown woman that I realized my lie had been weak and hadn't really fooled Mom.

EVERYBODY WAS MOVING to Cleveland after the coal mines started failing. The apartment we moved into was in a house on Cleveland's Hough Avenue. It had been a Jewish neighborhood, but with the mines failing and Blacks moving to Cleveland, it quickly became a neighborhood where whites owned and Blacks rented. Our Jewish landlords lived downstairs, and Johnny played with their eleven-year-old daughter, Arfa. Later, when I met Arfa as an adult, she would be a judge who gave me advice on how to deal with a serious case I caught.

I didn't realize I had never felt peace of mind until I was living with my mom and ten-year-old Johnny in a place without my father. The family was soon to grow. That year, at the age of eighteen, I got pregnant, even though I still had a lot to learn about my own body.

For most of my childhood I had tried to figure out so many things about sex, but nobody gave me the information. Grown people were thinking about World War II, but I had things that needed explaining, and no one seemed to want to explain them to me. I didn't even know what part of the bottom babies came out of. I thought they came out of the rectum, and I sure hadn't known that a woman bled every month before I started to.

One time, my oldest brother, Albert, had a girl in the back room of our house in Slab Fork, and he was going up and down under the covers. I had never seen anything like that, so I came on into the room and asked him, "Albert, what are you doing?" He jumped up right quick and yelled, "Run along!"

One Thanksgiving in Slab Fork, we were all seated

around the fire, cracking walnuts, and I rolled onto my stomach on the floor and started going up and down like my brother. Daddy said, "Dink, what's going on?" I figured somebody would tell me what I was doing, so I just kept doing it harder. I made that grunting noise my brother had made on top of that girl, until Mom and Daddy got up and went into the other room—I guess to discuss what to do with me. I went on back into it, just grunting and grunting, and when they came back out, I started going, "Uh-huh, oh yeah, baby yeah," figuring with all of that showing out, somebody was going to tell me something. Daddy dragged me by my hair all the way to my room. For a while, I had welts so big on my scalp that I couldn't even get my hair pressed. I had just wanted to show them what my brother had been doing and have somebody explain what I didn't understand.

I HAD ONE ally in helping me to decode things: Mr. Withers.

Mr. Withers was a Black man who was so light he looked white. He was the grandfather of the famous singer Bill Withers, who was just a little boy then, too little for me to play with. Mr. Withers owned a small store down the street that sold candy and ice cream.

One day my mom was sitting with her friends, and I walked into the room. She started spelling things as if I wasn't smart enough to figure out what she was spelling. She said, "Mrs. Dickson sure is"—and she spelled—"B-I-G." I knew what "big" meant, but I also knew they were talking about it in a way I didn't understand. I went and gave Mr. Withers the story I'd heard Mom telling. I told him I knew what "big" meant, but my mother had gone secretive on me with spelling "B-I-G." I waylaid Mr. Withers, trying to get an explanation out of him. I asked him, "What is this B-I-G stuff?" and he stretched out his arms around his belly. I asked him, "Like Mrs. Dickson?" who was gonna have a baby.

I went right to the table at dinner that evening and said in front of Mom and everybody, "Mrs. Dickson big, ain't she, Mom?" Mom was too through. She held her plate, glaring at me like I was a bad seed. I wanted my mom to know that I knew what they had been talking about, even though I still didn't understand it all and needed to know more. After that situation, though, Mr. Withers couldn't be bothered with any of my birds-and-bees questions. He would see me coming and cross to the other side of the road.

Finally, when I was twelve, I saw a woman walking down the street with her daughter who was "B-I-G," and I asked her, "How is that baby gonna come out of her?" She told me it was going to come out of her bottom. Well, that was something. All I could think of was how much shit it was going to have on it. I asked her, "If I take a laxative before I have a baby and get real cleaned out, will it still have doo-doo on it when it comes out?" She looked at me like I was crazy, and like Mr. Withers, she and her daughter walked away from me to avoid any more of my questions.

I THOUGHT I was never gonna have a baby and go through all that, but at eighteen I couldn't abstain anymore. I lay with a Black guy my age who also had lived in West Virginia. "Lay with" was the expression we used if the fella didn't have enough money for a hotel. He was in college and his father had an academic background. I didn't care anything about his status. I could support myself. I wasn't trying to catch a husband. After that, I just quit fucking. I didn't even like it anyway. I would lie there waiting for whatever was supposed to make me moan with pleasure like my brother and his girlfriend, and instead I would throw up before a fella could get off me.

The Phillis Wheatley house for single pregnant Black women was close to Mom's place on Hough. I wanted to show her that I could take care of myself, and that's where I got a real education about my body. Every night I was in somebody else's room, where we would sit around rubbing our bellies and educating ourselves from the pamphlets Mrs. Jane Edna Hunter gave us. These medical drawings showed us the difference between the rectum and the vagina. But the best education came from telling each other stories about having sex, and attempts at abstinence, and the horror stories we'd heard about abortions.

Like most of the girls, I got a job at Euclid Manor Nursing Home, my first and last normal job. The nursing home job became my front. I motivated myself through the pregnancy by using my money to purchase nice handbags, shoes, patterns for Mom to sew me nice dresses and suits—all the things to help me make a better life for myself, Mom, my brother Johnny, and my baby.

ONE EVENING AFTER dinner, I handed Mom a Butterick pattern for four beautiful linen dresses and a sophisticated suit. I rested my hand on my belly. "Can you make these for me?"

She sat back from the table and chuckled. I think most of my life I was a source of amusement for her. "Dink, look at your belly and look at the waistline on these patterns."

I told her, "These are for when I'm not pregnant. I have a plan."

"What plan?"

I didn't answer her. "Can you sew them for me?"

"Yes, but it's not my priority. I have sewing I do for a living, you know." She rarely got stern with me, but sometimes I could see that she just got fed up dealing with whatever was going on in my scheming head.

I needed to look monied up, to represent wealth that exceeded the white woman's, to play the part that made it easy to steal. I had learned the behavior and manners at home, from Mom's refined upbringing, the tools that exhibited good breeding, and gained an understanding of fashion from the magazines I studied. When Louise and I were kids, Mom bought us little embroidery kits, and we made nice things when we could no longer buy them. A fine handbag and shoes could define everything, but I couldn't tell her I was begging her to make me a jewel thief costume.

I NAMED MY baby Ronald. His father didn't live with us, but he came around to see the baby. I moved back in with Mom, and we worked together to raise Ronald. Ronald's other grandmother was a big help too. She was a really nice woman who lived in Akron, Ohio, who would take the baby often.

I thought I was going to get right down to my jewel thief plan, but being a new mother with my first child kept me so busy that half the time I didn't know morning from night. I wasn't with Ronald's father anymore, but a couple of times he came by and we got tight with each other. When Ronald was about to turn four years old, I told his father I was pregnant again. He laughed because he saw how I always vomited right after lying with him.

We thought about getting married, but I didn't ever want to get married. I believed and still believe it's wise for women to accept being in love but to assume the responsibility of providing for themselves. That married piece of paper just ties you to brutality. I told him I was too scared to have an abortion because Black women didn't survive abortions. I had heard many stories of girls bleeding out in some back room. There I was getting B-I-G. A few months later, my daughter, Rhonda, was born.

I stayed in training while Rhonda was little. Once my belly was nice and flat again, Mom finally agreed to make me a handful of dresses and suits.

One day I carried one of my dresses to work on the bus in a suit bag. I had a white girlfriend, Norma, who was from Beckley. We weren't best friends or anything, but she kept complaining to me at lunchtime that she was having trouble affording the cost of her mother's medicine. I was having trouble getting all the accessories for the jobs I wanted to do. I cooked up a plan to take some shit and give her a cut of the money. At lunchtime, we ducked into the nurses' bathroom to get changed. I fancied her up in one of the dresses Mom had made. I kept my uniform on, and we went farther down Euclid to the May Company department store. We had to hurry up because lunch wasn't but forty-five minutes long.

We took the elevator to jewelry and accessories. We kept our arms linked. I told her, "Slump over a bit and look like one of those waify Victorian heiresses." I put on a stern nurse's face. We walked like that up to the jewelry counter, and I spoke for my rich, sickly patient. "Good morning. Miss Rockford would like to see your wedding sets. She is soon to be married and hopes to have some say over what the groom purchases."

The clerk was a kind-looking older guy. He softened even more watching Norma tremble trying on rings. I almost cracked up. She was really playing the part.

Twice he said, "Here, let me help." I was waiting for him to say, "What's wrong with her?" but this dude thought whoever was marrying her shaky ass was sure doing it for the money. He got to yes ma'amin' and no ma'amin' and pulling all manner of things out of the case for my wealthy, young sickly patient, who was really a poor white coal miner's daughter. I kept my arm around her waist and gave her a little tweak to say, *Take the damned thing. We got to go.* Finally, while the clerk was bent down into the case, I said, "Here, Miss Rockford. Let me help you." I slipped a band and small diamond wedding ring into her dress pocket. "Sorry, sir, we'll have to come back tomorrow. Miss Rockford isn't feeling well."

We took a cab back to work, and she kept saying, "Oh my God!" with her hand over her mouth. I recognized those big watery eyes from when Lil first saw me trick the Woolworth's man. I couldn't have anybody messing around in my shit, especially if they had the diamond fever. I gave her $100 and told her I'd get rid of the piece at a pawnshop. "That was a onetime thing, Norma. I just needed to help you get your mother some medicine, but we can't do that again." I let her think she was the one tainting me. "I'm sorry to put you in that situation, Doris. Thank you."

Of course I was thinking, *Bye, Norma, and bye, Euclid Manor.* The wedding set was worth around $1,500—the equivalent of $14,000 today. The next week, I bought myself a mauve and green purse, a hat, and a pair of shoes to match. I couldn't believe I still had $1,300 left. I carried myself down to a different pawnshop and bought a wedding set better-looking than the one I stole, a round-cut diamond in a gold prong setting with a gold band with tiny inlaid diamonds. With my accessories and the dresses Mom sewed, I looked like a married, monied woman of class. I had the whole outfit and was done wiping old people's butts for a living.

CHAPTER 7

MY FIRST BIG HEIST

OUT IN THE KITCHEN, MY BROTHER JOHNNY and my children admired my outfit. "Ooooo!" and "Ooo wee, Mama." I grabbed a piece of toast and caught Mom's sideways glace. She brought the skillet of eggs over to the table and looked up and down at the handiwork of her sewing turned elegant on my frame, the purse and the shoes, and the jewelry that lied about me being married. I pulled my white gloves over my hands and tossed a wink at my children.

"Eat some breakfast, Dink," Mom said, and squinted at me the way she had when she'd peeked through the slats of the woodshed back in West Virginia, where I'd played make-believe and beat up on my imaginary husband the way I saw Daddy beat up on her. His black coal-dirty fists would connect with her sun-toasted skin. She had watched me beat the shit out of my made-up husband to get back at Daddy.

"I'm fine with toast, Mom."

She stood there with the skillet, deciding if she was gonna say something. Johnny gobbled his breakfast to keep up with the clock and get his bus. Ronny didn't have to be at school for another hour and Rhonda was Mom's charge for the day. They took advantage of me and Mom standing there staring at each other. They slathered way too much jelly on their toast. I sent Mom the message with my stare that I was going to get us out of this cold-ass apartment that smelled like city-bus fumes. I would get us out just like I got us out of that coal miner's company house where Dad kept her prisoner.

She broke the silence. "Dink, where are you headed looking like that on a Friday morning? You need to get yourself together and get to work."

"I have some business to do in Pittsburgh." I saw the heft of her chest deflate as she turned back to the stove and decided not to ask me any more.

I TURNED HEADS as I arrived at the bus station in downtown Cleveland. The admiration I received all along the way boosted my confidence a bit even though I kept looking at my reflection in the shop windows, thinking, *Who do you think you are? Here you are about to catch a bus dressed like you should be stepping into a limousine.*

I sat on the Greyhound bus in my good clothes for the

two and a half hours. I watched Cleveland fade behind me, and some part of my childhood, teenage years, and early twenties faded behind me for good. At twenty-six years old, I spent every day wiping old white people's butts, letting them think I was just who they needed me to be—some Black woman who rode in the back of the bus each morning like every other Black Cleveland woman headed to her subservient job. But on weekends, I was Doris Payne, jewel thief in training. I was still perfecting my ways—don't get me wrong, I was no amateur, by no means—but I was well on my way to becoming who I wanted to be: a master jewel thief of international renown.

The bus crossed the bridge over the Ohio River into Pittsburgh. The countrywomen traveling with me put their bonnets on. Farmers pinched their hats and set them back on their heads. And the finer white women, dressed not much different from me, fetched their feathered hats from the racks above.

I got fever in my skin and jittered in my suit jacket. Part of me was thinking, *You've practiced this*, and part of me was thinking, *Girl, you lost your mind*. I hadn't made a plan for if I got caught. I wouldn't make that mistake in the future. What if my ass ended up in prison? I had only trained and practiced for the heist at hand—I knew to ask to see several rings, to talk the clerk to pure distraction, all the while doing three-card-monte moves with the rings until I was wearing one more than I entered the store wearing. *What if I get caught?*

I quickly let those thoughts rise up into the smog as the bus passed through the narrow streets of Pittsburgh. My mind had to be clear for me to be successful at getting the jewel. All I could hear in my head now was the bopping beat of Chuck Berry, crooning *"Oh, Maybellene, why can't you be true?"*

After I got off the bus, I put my gloves on, hung my handbag over my forearm, pinned my hat to my head, and strolled four blocks down Liberty Avenue like I was in the Easter parade. They had fixed up the Clark Building. MGM Studios had taken over the top floors. But the second floor was where the finest jewelers catered to movie stars coming and going from the building.

I stood in front of the gold-plated elevator doors with the marble walls surrounding them and left behind any thought of being lesser. I was somebody famous. I was Doris Payne.

A doorman stood in front of one of the shops in a narrow black suit. "Good morning, madam." His smile lured me away from another jeweler. I smiled back and watched his eyes. He had that starstruck look that is some combination of eager to please and stupid. He waved his hand forward, welcoming me into the place. The glare of the chandeliers cast rainbows from every diamond in the store. This is called diamond fire and is like candy to the eyes of a jewel thief. Mahogany cases were positioned around the store in a U shape. They contained necklaces, watches, all displayed on velvety red cloth. Then I saw the case with the rings, and I exhaled because I knew this was it. My entire body tingled.

I held my head up in proper lady fashion, but my eyes scanned everything in the store. I looked to see if there was a security guard. No. There were two clerks. Two white women shoppers were at the other cases with their backs to me. One woman had on a light-green tapered-below-the-knee skirt and a matching short-sleeved jacket. Similar to my outfit, but hers was accessorized with a belt and a cute black pillbox hat. I liked the look and took a mental note. The other woman was younger and wore a pink-rose-colored linen short-sleeved dress. She also wore a pillbox hat and draped a lightweight white shawl around her shoulders. I could see that my outfit was on par with theirs, confirming I looked the part. I was glad there were other customers. It would be easier to confuse the two clerks if their attention was divided. One of the clerks was assisting the two women, and the bald clerk came to me. "What can I help you with today?"

I kept my air about me, my body not revealing my inner nervousness—my mental state was warring with my physical appearance—and I said in my most proper tone, "I am interested in a two-carat diamond. Something beautiful for evening attire."

I could see his eyes shift with excitement at my request. He motioned the other clerk over and guided me to a set of two chairs covered in paisley fabric facing each other at a small mahogany table. The two pillboxes did their niceties and left the store, leaving the other salesman to seem attentive to nothing. So he brought the bald clerk and me a tray of rings that ranged between $5,000 and $20,000. My ring was the $20,000 piece on the tray. That's equivalent to about $187,000 now.

I was thinking, *Ooo Baby Jesus!* But I maintained that upward tilt of my head and kept my legs crossed and my hands folded over my knees.

I was relaxed. This was the fun I remembered as a teenager making store clerks forget what they were doing. I started my three-card-monte shuffle with the rings—tried on the ring I desired, I took it off, I tried on another, I took that off, I tried on others, I moved it to the other hand, I took two and put both on one finger at a time, I took one off and put it on the other hand, looked at both hands, held one hand up and put the other one on my lap, and I sometimes "accidentally" got my wedding ring mixed up in the mess. That made the two of us laugh. I got to telling him a funny story about taking off my rings once to wash my hands and losing my diamond engagement ring down the drain. "Ohh, my plumber had an *awful* time trying to retrieve it before my husband arrived home from the firm." I could see him becoming more excited about the sale, as he was getting more confused about what he was doing. Finally, he called for two trays and hadn't yet returned the first one. I knew it was time to slip the big rectangular-shaped rock onto my finger. Like a cashier not wanting his drawer to come up short at closing, he would spend the rest of the day looking for the missing ring. He would wait to tell his manager about his carelessness, and I would be long gone.

We laughed and blushed and carried on like that until I

was ready to go. I thanked him graciously, said I would talk over the purchase with my husband but would surely come back in the morning.

My heart wasn't even beating fast. I was still in character. I smiled charmingly as I passed the doorman, slipping my gloves on. My nose was elevated much higher. I stayed that way until my feet hit the concrete of the Pittsburgh sidewalks. My heart started beating hard in my chest. It was all I could do not to start running and laughing out loud. On my finger, under my white glove, was a $20,000 diamond ring. I felt ecstatic. I had pulled off my biggest job to date. My mind was racing with dreams of what I could provide for my family.

CHAPTER 8

HOT ICE, COLD FEET

WALKING DOWN THE STREETS OF PITTS-burgh to get to the bus station, I kept my stride with my head held high and the air that had convinced that jeweler that he had a sale, not a swindle. I could see women looking at me, and men checking me out. I was still confident.

Then I turned the corner and saw a cop standing there. I froze for a split second, looked at him, and he looked directly at me. Then I continued my stride, walking as I had been before—because I dared not run. *Oh shit. Did that salesclerk discover the missing ring already?* I hurried along my way. I needed to get the hell out of there.

Once I got back to the bus station, all of a sudden my plan for getting home seemed downright silly, and then a panic began to set in. *Surely the police will come for me while I'm waiting to hop a Greyhound and head back to Cleveland.* I needed to think fast—and act even faster.

I walked up to the ticket counter line and turned around. *Maybe I should change clothes.* But I hadn't brought a change of clothes. I went into the bathroom, took off my gloves, fidgeted the diamond ring off my finger, and put it in the cup of my bra.

There hadn't ever been anything I'd done wrong that Mom didn't forgive me for, so I went to the pay phone and called her. It was noon, and she was probably making lunch for Rhonda. She didn't answer. Then I remembered she had said she was going to walk Rhonda to the park. I waited a while and called again at one p.m. She didn't answer. I tried again, and she picked up, "Shhh, I just got Rhonda to take a nap." She had a little edge in her voice, like she wanted to yell at me but couldn't. This sure wouldn't be the time to tell her I had gotten myself into some shit. I told her I'd be home soon.

I called three more times wanting to tell her the truth, but ended up talking small talk until finally I heard Rhonda in the background, "Nanna! Nanna!"

Mom did the best she could not to yell, "Get your ass home, Dink!"

It was three o'clock and the boys would be home from school any minute. Hesitating made it worse. I just kept looking at the ticket counter thinking as soon as I walked up there the police were going to pop up out of nowhere and grab me.

Every time anyone in any sort of dark-colored uniform walked through the station, I thought I would have a heart attack. I went back to the bathroom because it seemed better than being out in the open.

I riffled through my purse, counting the last of my money. I'd spent so much on my anxious phone calls that I didn't have enough for the bus ticket anymore. I'd really blown it. I stood in a bathroom stall and removed the ring from my bra to inspect my diamond. It wasn't cone shaped with lots of tiny cuts around the top that created a beautiful sparkle of colors. What if it was a fake? It was long and rectangular with a few cuts around the edges that stepped it down in the setting. I kept angling it in the yellow lighting, trying to get it to sparkle, but nothing. Feeling a bit disappointed with myself, I put the ring back in my bra.

I wasn't yet sophisticated enough to know that this was an emerald-cut diamond, and the rarest sort of cut, because in its raw form it had the most amount of clear space. It was the most expensive type of diamond in the world. It was clear, beautiful, pulled right from the heart of Africa. But I was a jewel thief in training and didn't know any of that standing in a bathroom stall with my confidence fading.

Night fell, and I was exhausted. In the bathroom there was a little bathtub and shower enclosed in one of the stalls. I neatly rolled my suit jacket to use for a pillow and curled up in the tub, figuring it would be like Mom used to say— "Easier to know what's right after a good night's sleep." This meant I would be gone overnight and Mom would be worried about whether I was all right. I didn't know what else to do. I fell asleep with the ring pinching my left breast.

WHEN I WOKE UP, there was a big broad-legged white woman who worked at the station standing over me, yelling, "Get the hell out of here!"

I tried to jump to my feet, but I had been curled up in that bathtub all night. I couldn't straighten up right. I got to my feet and went to the sink to get myself together. She glared a warning, looked me up and down, and left me there to figure out my shit. I used one of Mom's old techniques. In the summertime in West Virginia, it was too hot to go standing over an iron. So she would put a little water on her hands, smooth her hands over the wrinkles, and when the garment dried, she was wrinkle-free. I got to smoothing water on my jacket and skirt. For a while, I walked hunchbacked around the station, all messed up, waiting to dry without wrinkles. I struggled down the steps, all crippled-looking. People were probably thinking, *Who is this young, well-dressed Black woman looking like she has some problem?*

I was hungry. I had to figure out how to get grub covered, and how to recoup the money I'd spent on phone calls so I could buy a ticket home. The station was busy. I noticed several military buses with inductees reporting for duty. A good number of enlisted Black men were roaming the station. I came up with a plan. I sat next to a handsome, clean-cut fellow in uniform who was not much older than my teenaged brother Johnny. I smiled at him and reversed drag on this dude.

I asked him, "Can I buy you a cup of coffee?" I didn't even have a nickel to spare for my own cup of coffee, but I got a big cinnamon roll full of nuts and raisins and some coffee, and he got himself something too. My plan was to pretend to exit and have him say, "Don't worry, sweetheart, I got this." When he left his money for the bill, I'd take it.

Just when I was about to get up, they called him for his bus, and he didn't have time to pay. I thought, *I've blown some shit now.*

I had just stolen an expensive diamond ring, didn't know what to do with it, didn't have enough money to get home, didn't know what reprimand waited for me at home, and now this. During the three hours I'd spent fidgeting and figuring, I remembered my old tricks from the days the coal miners went on strike and my family didn't have enough money to buy even a piece of fatback. My move was all about the market clerk's work break.

As soon as the shift changed and the waitresses changed, I got the hell out of there. I didn't get on the bus, because I still didn't have enough for a ticket. I hurried back into the bathroom, took the ring out of my bra, and put it back on my finger to transform back into a movie star.

I walked back toward the Clark Building, thinking maybe I'd just take the ring back. Maybe I could say some lie, that I had been partying all night with my movie castmates and noticed I still had it on. That would explain me being in the same clothes and would get me out of that shit before it was too late. I could call Mom and not have to lie when I told her I went to Pittsburgh for the day, spent too much money on phone calls, and needed somebody to help me get home.

It was Saturday morning. The fog hadn't lifted yet. I took a glance at myself in every store window I passed and straightened my spine. I put my white gloves back on. That's when I passed a store called Rahall, with a doorman. In the display window was a fine gold-lamé robe.

In that moment, I didn't figure out what to do; I knew what to do.

I held my head up and checked his eyes to see if they bucked open like he'd spotted a wanted criminal. He just smiled and said, "Good morning."

I smiled back and told myself, *Come on, Doris, get it together.* The walls were high, like palace walls. A man in a suit was playing classical music on a violin in the corner of the shop.

A brunette woman with flawless skin walked toward me in a dress tied at the waist. She grinned so wide I could tell she thought I was someone famous. I think everybody did because of the way I carried myself. I was a looker and knew it. The woman asked, "How can I help you today?"

I matched her wispy tone. "I love that robe in the window."

She walked me to a rack with four of them. I took off my

gloves and separated the robes with my hand and took note of each of the sizes: 4, 6, 10, 12. I pulled the size 6 from the rack, making sure to flash the emerald-cut diamond.

"Do you have the robe in an eight?"

Of course she didn't. She blurted out, "What a beautiful ring!"

I looked at her woefully, as if her comment had reminded me of some tragedy. I pulled a handkerchief from my purse and cried the tears of a woman in distress. In some ways, I was distressed. I had just stolen a diamond ring, and I had no clue who was onto me, and I couldn't get my ass home unless I sold the piece. I cried even louder. "I'm recently divorced, and this is the last piece of jewelry I'm in the process of selling. I can't be reminded any longer of my husband and his affairs with other actresses."

She took over. She comforted me and left me at ease in a chair. She went and got a tall, older, gray-haired white man in a gray suit who carried himself as the manager of the place. He had a confident air, almost hard, and his eyes looked at me dead-on. He didn't say very much. I got the impression this dude was familiar with a side hustle or two.

He took a little sterling-silver magnifying glass out of his pocket to look at the ring. He said in a deep, calm tone, "What do you want for it?"

I had no clue. The price tag had said $20,000 when I took it, and I didn't know if it was real because it didn't sparkle. I had to tell him something. I couldn't go letting the whole thing fall through now. I had to figure out what to charge for it. After my eighth-grade education in West Virginia, I had learned everything from reading the newspaper, including world geography and the stock market. Dividing by three to figure out the depreciated worth made logical sense to me. So I divided by three, which I got to doing because I figured at least three people had owned it at some point before me: the Africans who had gotten it out of the ground, much like the coal miners in West Virginia; the people who bought raw diamonds on the black market; and the people in Brussels who got rich by mutilating diamonds, polishing them, and standing them on an auction block for European trade.

Anyway, I sure couldn't tell the man to hold on a second so I could go run out on the street and ask somebody, "Hey, can you help me figure out how to sell this ring I stole?"

So I told him, with my eyes still streaming tears, "I'll sell it for seven thousand dollars."

He looked up from the piece and met my eyes, and I couldn't read his expression. "Okay."

He went into the back room and came out with $7,000 in cash—about $65,000 today. *What the hell!* I had never seen that much money in my life, but I couldn't let on. He stacked it and put it in an envelope like he had done this plenty of times. As I suspected, this dude knew a side hustle. The envelope fit perfectly in my empty mauve and green purse.

THE AIR OUTSIDE had warmed up. The sun was making its way through the smog. I breathed in deep, took off my jacket with a bop in my step, and held my smile until I could get some distance from the store. Then I laughed out loud.

Hell with the bus. I took a cab all the way to Cleveland.

I gave the cabdriver a $10 bill, and over the Ohio River we went with Chuck Berry blasting on the radio, "*Oh, Maybellene, why can't you be true? You done started back doing the things you used to do.*"

I laughed so hard, rocking in that cab, till it seemed it would turn over into the river. I was cackling and thinking, *What you think now, Mr. Benjamin?*

CHAPTER 9

MAKING GOOD ON
MY CRIMES

THAT SHOP OWNER IN PITTSBURGH HAD PUT $7,000 into my mauve and green purse, cash money for my diamond. This wasn't no nickel-and-dime shit. I was becoming as good at getting people's money as the men on Wall Street. I was moving up the ladder. But I didn't want to go anywhere in life without my mother. I was ready to tell her.

I sat out on the steps of our porch the day after the Pittsburgh heist and smoked a cigarette. Each time I exhaled, it set me deeper in a satisfied confidence that I could take care of my family. From the open window, Ella Fitzgerald crooned. Mom's favorite album was perfect for dusk. I looked up and down Hough Avenue, a long way from Slab Fork Road but not far enough. I had proved I could do it and now it was time for more of what we deserved. No more duplex apartment with warped windows and hissing radiators. I squished the cigarette under my new black flats and called to her from the porch. "Can you come sit out here with me?"

She left the kids inside and came and sat awhile. Night was coming on fast, and the street was quieting down. Folks were having their supper and enjoying a warm spring Sunday night out on their porches. Ella serenaded, *"Pennies in a stream, falling leaves, a sycamore."*

"Dink, you better not come in my house smoking."

I smiled, swaying to the music. I lit up another cigarette, and Mom waved her hands, and the both of us laughed. "Sorry about that," I said, and waved the smoke away from her.

I didn't hesitate. I wanted to feel all the way free, to have the weight lifted and have her with me as I moved further into my profession. "Mom, I take jewelry and resell it. That's how I get money to take care of us."

She didn't respond, just sat there on the stoop expressionless.

"I'm really good at it and have been doing it for a while." I turned to look at her and regretted not turning on the porch light. I put my half-smoked cigarette out and waited. She still didn't say a word. My eyes adjusted as the streetlights came on. She didn't look mad or sad or change her face at all. She just watched it get dark and then got up and went into the house. She turned the porch light on me like a searchlight. I saw her peeking out the window at me like she was checking to see if I was crazy.

After a bit, I came on in. The kids were in bed. I could hear the landlord upstairs clunking around. Each night they put Arfa to bed and packed up a few things. They were among the last Jews in the neighborhood. All of their brothers had split their homes into apartments and rented to the Black people who wouldn't stop pouring in from the South.

Mom sat at the table with just the dim bulb over the sink to light the kitchen. The Ella album reached its end. I heard the mechanical clicking of the needle arm as it picked up and lay down again, and the music restarted. This wasn't going how I had imagined it. I had thought her eyes would light up at knowing we would never be broke, that I could handle it. I came around and sat across from her. "I'm not stealing. I'm taking."

She searched my eyes in the dim light. "Don't let the kids find out you're 'taking'—they'll think it's right before God to do it too."

I scooted my chair back from her with attitude. "Mom, it's right before God to take care of yourself and not let somebody else control what you can and cannot have, even if it means taking what nobody is gonna give you."

She laughed out loud. "'Taking'? You mean stealing."

I raised my voice. "I mean taking."

"Dink, if it ain't stealing, what is it? Calling it something else don't make it something else."

I knew I could never win a fight with Mom. She would say the true thing that I wasn't ready to see in myself and then everything else I said after that would sound childish.

I defended, raising my voice. "Mom, diamonds come out of mines. Africans work the mines."

Mom squinted then let out an exasperated laugh. She waved her hand, skootched up her housedress, got up quick, and left me in the kitchen to figure myself out.

I couldn't sit there in all of that confusion when I had been feeling confident and satisfied. I took my smokes and walked the neighborhood.

Lights were on in the apartments. There were occasional sounds from a radio, laughter, or muffled conversation coming from the open windows. Two blocks over, there were uniform brick houses, all one floor, with a little A-frame attic on top. All the lights on that block were already out. One of the houses had a white poster in the yard. I walked over to read it: FOR SALE. I recognized the phone number under it as our landlord's.

The next morning our conversation was simple. I asked him if I could buy it. I didn't know anything about buying houses. He said, "Cash on the barrelhead." I knew what that meant, and we looked at each other for a while, acknowledging that he knew something about what I had been up to and didn't care as long as I gave him cash money for the purchase. I rode with him to the bank in his big ole black Imperial. *Lord, if Mom saw me riding with this man, she would snatch a knot in my head.*

I stood there in my green linen dress with my nose in the air, my $7,000 from the emerald-cut diamond in Pittsburgh in my purse. The notary came over. She squeezed the deed between a clamp and signed, then my landlord signed, and in the place of "Buyer," I signed the deed.

When Mom got home from work, she didn't ask one question when I said, "Let's take a walk." We walked a couple of blocks over to where the houses were not split into apartments. In front of each brick home there was just enough space for a little lawn and a flower bed. Each with porches so much the same that you could stand on one porch and see down the block like looking through a tunnel.

We stood in front of the four-bedroom brick house that had the FOR SALE sign on the lawn. I pulled the sign out of the ground.

"Dink, what in the world are you doing?"

I wanted her to see the things I hadn't managed to say at the kitchen table. "I bought you, Johnny, and my kids a house."

She gave me that look I'd seen so many times, the look of peeking through the slats of the shed—just before she smiled.

I WAS HIGH on what I had done for my mom. I was ready to take another big piece. The next week, on a Tuesday just before four p.m., I got a cab to Halle's, the tallest, most upscale department store on Euclid Avenue. I knew the store closed on weekdays at five p.m. I knew closing time or break time was great for catching the clerks when they were ready to be done working and might be more likely to get careless. I knew this store was where I had seen the blue-vein elite Blacks of Cleveland shop, the same ones who played tennis and hosted debutante balls for their daughters. They were all light-skinned like me, and I had studied the way the young women dressed.

I wore the green short-sleeved linen dress again. I had a black belt around my waist, a nice black leather purse, and black leather tiny-heeled pumps. My hair was perfectly pressed with a little flip at the edges. Conservative and elegant. To top it all off, I wore a debutante ring. A few days earlier, after a long conversation with a jeweler about the latest rings for young ladies, I had taken it for my outfit even though I thought it was ugly.

I stepped off the elevator into the fine accessories department. The lighting of small cut-glass chandeliers made any woman who got off that elevator look ready for a movie-star close-up. I walked over to the handbags and took a look at the Chanel and Vuitton bags on display. I never looked around like an owl twisting my head this way and that when I walked through a shop. I smiled at the clerks. I counted two female clerks in the handbags section. There was one female customer in a black overcoat pushing a pram. Her diamond bracelet noticeably caught the light, and her cooing baby caught the attention of the two clerks.

I strolled over to the jewelry counter, the only place on the floor where a man stood. He wore typical attire, a black suit that was slightly ill-fitting. I found myself making alterations with my eyes to have the jacket fit more snugly against his frame and make him look more muscular and less fat. He didn't quite fit the part of a man who sold fine jewelry. They always wore tailored suits. It concerned me that he looked more disheveled than clerks I'd dealt with in other stores. His tie wasn't tied quite right, and I could see the folds of skin around his neck. Something in me had the feeling I was dealing with a redneck dressed up like a fine-jewelry clerk. I told myself to quit overthinking it and get to work. On approach, I smiled, and he smiled. He remarked, "Good evening, ma'am."

Okay, he is smiling and called me ma'am. I know my outfit is on par. I'm ready to work. I saw him make a triangle with his eyes on my debutante ring, my necklace with the one teardrop-shaped diamond, and my eyes, which were still smiling at him. He blushed. I knew this would be easy.

We proceeded with the dance of conversation against my better judgment.

He told me his name was Fred. He mentioned his family was from North Carolina, and I noticed a coffee stain on his white sleeve. Part of me said, *Doris, just abort this mission,* but I already had him chatting so much about his brother who sold insurance and his niece who was the family's pride as a graduate of Meredith College in Raleigh, North Carolina. He again noticed my debutante ring, which had three tiny diamonds set on each side of a small emerald. He held my hand, and I wanted to puke because his hand was wet and clammy, but I knew to smile charmingly.

"This is a beautiful ring," he said, and he went on about his niece again. "Deborah has an alumni ring. The first graduating class to get such a beautiful memento."

I smiled this time for real. His niece was a familiar place for us to continue the chatting and for me to induce confusion. He went on at length about her ring. I took off my debutante ring, placed on a ring, and began my game of switch-up. I saw his eyes grow weary but his mouth kept moving. I pointed at something else in the case, and he took out another tray. He had ten pieces out of the case, way more pieces than anyone in their right mind would ever have out at once.

The lights blinked, indicating the store was about to close. I said, "Oh my goodness. My father will be waiting in the car to pick me up." We frantically collected the rings from the counter. I was still wearing one he had shown me, and I also put on my debutante ring. "I'll be back with my father tomorrow to purchase." As I turned to go, I knew he was watching me walk. I turned back before getting on the elevator, and said, "Congratulations to your niece."

I was out of the store with the piece hailing a cab when a police car pulled up. I saw prison flash before my eyes. A tall white male officer got out like he was truly a cabdriver. He respectfully opened the back door of his patrol car and said, "Get in, miss."

I complied even though part of me wanted to run. He pulled away, and I asked, "Has one of my parents been in an accident?"

I saw his smirk in the rearview mirror.

"No, young lady. A store clerk called and said a female nigger in a green dress took some jewelry."

I gasped like a woman in distress and clutched my teardrop necklace.

"Oh my goodness." I heard a little Scarlett O'Hara come out of my accent. "We tried on so many rings I still have one on." I hung my open hand over the front seat with the ring on it. He left my hand dangling there until he pulled over. I brightened up my lie before he could speak. "Things were closing up. He forgot to take this one off. Oh my, I forgot to give it to him." I didn't want to do too much more explaining, just a little, just enough to get me out of that shit. When lying, you don't want to overdo it. The less explanation the better.

He turned to look at me, and I knew he was assessing the situation. I knew I had to sell the blue-vein thing. I was so nervous. But I put it all into my act. "I completely forgot I was wearing it. I know father is going to be picking out a graduation present for me. I guess I shouldn't have been trying to pick out a gift ahead of time." I had never in my life had a police officer talk to me other than Mr. Buster Foster, who was the policeman who walked our street as his beat in Slab Fork. He was a white man, but the kids would run to him, asking him to help them find their lost wagon or lost dog. One time I asked him to arrest my parents because they were trying to make me eat slop. He thought I was amusing.

But this tall, stern Cleveland police officer wasn't no

Mr. Buster Foster. He just glared at me, and I wanted to vomit, thinking about the way Mom was going to glare at me too when she had to pick me up from the police station. He studied the distraught look in my eyes. He assessed my outfit and my debutante ring, which I had on the hand that lay open with the stolen ring in it. I think he realized that my own jewels and my clothes were more valuable than the ring. I saw his brow relax.

He took the ring out of my hand and told me, "You watch yourself, young lady." Then he said, "Let me get you a cab."

I learned something new in my training that day: if I walked out of a store "forgetting" I was wearing the ring and they caught me, I could just give it back and let them know that Fred, or whoever was calling me a nigger, had forgotten what he was doing, which was true. I could tell them that I also had forgotten, which wasn't true but was certainly plausible. They would take one look at my clothing and class status and let me go. It would be over.

THIS WORKED FOR a few more small heists in downtown Cleveland. One day I read about one of the pieces I had taken in the crime section of the local rag. The store reported the ring I took as valued at $5,000 when the price tag had actually said $1,500.

I read up and found out that in order to keep their insurance, jewelers were only supposed to have five or fewer pieces out of their cases at a time. If they had more out and somehow lost one through any means, they were shy about reporting that to the police, who would send a report of the store's negligence to their insurance company. Getting a piece back when the mistake was theirs was worse than reporting the loss. Many of the stores were glad the piece was never found. Then they could report the loss as much higher than the value of the piece. *Those damned crooks.* They would take hours or days reconstructing the truth to keep their insurance from going through the roof, and to get more than the ring was worth. This, I realized, was one of the reasons why I hadn't been picked up before.

I was playing a game of Russian roulette by taking things right there in town and selling them at a local pawnshop. This pattern would result in a case if I didn't figure out how to make their shadiness work in favor of my shadiness.

I had to practice making it their fault. I couldn't take anything unless they had more than five pieces out of a case. I also needed to know how to sell the valuable jewels without it being traceable to me. I was getting out of my league. I needed more knowledge of the streets and of the black market to figure it all out.

CHAPTER 10

TAKING THINGS TO THE NEXT LEVEL

I MET A JEWISH WOMAN NAMED ADA LURCH IN THE Woolworth's on Euclid one day. She thought I looked hip, and I thought she was a real interesting woman. And she was fashionable—my kind of woman. She wore bright-yellow sling-back pumps with a two-inch heel. My feet were a narrow size 7 with no arch. Anything that high that didn't hug the back of my foot was out of the question. I appreciated her yellow suit too, and the strange beauty of wearing a fox fur and a red hat with all of that color. We struck up a conversation. She told me she had gotten out of jail and was having some legal problems because she owned a whorehouse on the west side. I had never heard of no shit like that. But if she trusted me enough to talk about her crimes, she could be someone I could open up to.

When I told her I was about to engage in some high-stakes criminal activity and didn't know how to get rid of the shit quick, Ada said, "Go to 105 Saint Clair Avenue. I know an Israeli Jew named Babe. A lot of pro baseball players are there on Mondays when his nightclub is closed. Babe gets them hookers and stuff, and he'll be able to connect you with some serious buyers."

She told me his real name was Harold Bronfield, but everybody who knew him called him "Babe." She spoke highly of him. He had been the first Jewish boy to go to Alabama State. "He's well connected with a lot of politicians and monied athletes, honey. He's also as well connected to the shady side as you can get." She repeated, "Go on Monday."

It was Thursday. I had time to prepare.

I stared at a photo of a piece in *Charm* magazine. My plan was to head to Birks & Sons in the financial district in Montreal, Canada, and pick it up. I took a deep breath. This Babe fellow was well connected. I had to be all show, not all talk. This would be the first time I left the country, but I told myself not to think about that. *Get there, get the piece, and get home.*

At the time, you didn't need a passport to go shopping in Montreal for the day. I caught an overnight bus to New York City, hired a driver, and crossed the border into Montreal that morning in a black Fleetwood. It was fall 1957. The change in the crisp air fascinated me. The landscape was as flat as I had ever seen. When we pulled into the city, there were so many old brick buildings, old cathedrals and churches with stone arches and high buttresses. These were the images I had studied in school.

I told myself to focus. I was wearing a long-sleeved turquoise dress tapered down just below my knee, a belt to match tied at the waist to show off my figure, and a pair of black low-heel pumps, and I carried a fine black leather handbag. Inside my black gloves was my diamond wedding and engagement set.

The car pulled up in front of a building with a big ole open iron door with spikes on it and a big clock over the top of the door. The driver came around and assisted me. I took another deep breath and got into movie-star confidence before I stepped out of the black Fleetwood onto the sidewalk.

Those white Canadians on the street fawned over the monied Black woman. They whispered to each other, "Who is that?" The doorman took off his hat and had those same fawning eyes. The clerk who met me at the door had a smile all lit up by the store's chandeliers. This place had round pillars in the middle like the Colosseum or some shit. There were high wooden cases, and green crushed velvet covered the wooden chairs. I noticed the glass jewelry cases, with even more lights. This was high class.

I walked into the store with my lips pursed and my head up. There were two female customers shopping alone, three couples who looked like European tourists, and one Arab-looking man. A perfect number of people to make my job quick and easy.

The male clerk stuttered, "Wh-what would you like to

see today?" I spun him quickly into a conversation about fine clubs and music in New York City, which at the time I didn't know much about, but he didn't know that. When he blushed and looked away, I knew I had him. The confusion was my next step. I mentioned twice that my driver was waiting to take me on to other shopping, which made him eager for a sale. I took off my wedding set and tried on rings. I said, "I hope I'll have enough time today to do more shopping."

He got watery mouthed for a quick sale and broke his own rule. He brought out an additional tray. After a moment of laughs and ring swapping, I told him I would think about the purchase. I slipped my gloves on with the ring under and left out the same door. The doorman tipped his hat and said, "Have a good day," almost bowing.

I nearly cracked up at that.

It was as simple as swiping a loaf of bread. On my finger under my gloves was a two-carat round diamond ring surrounded by a halo setting of tiny blue sapphire stones that I "forgot" I was wearing.

The driver kept his head erect and eyes on the road as we drove back to New York. He let me out of the car. I walked through the front door of the Waldorf Astoria. I asked to use the ladies' room, put the ring in my bra, and walked back out.

On the bus ride back to Cleveland, I watched the stars brighten against the dark sky. I imagined how things must have gone after I left Birks & Sons. I could see the clerk looking for the piece for a while, embarrassed that he hadn't figured out it was gone. He'd wait until the close of business, then call the store owner. All the while wondering if he should tell the truth about breaking the rule of five. The bus was comfortable. I was exhausted, but I slept like a queen.

MONDAY AFTERNOON I went to meet Babe to demonstrate that I knew what I was doing before I attempted to enter into an arrangement with him to sell my high-end stuff to his high-end contacts. This screaming piece would vouch for me.

The inside of the club was dimly lit in the middle of the day. On the stage in the back were some Black musicians, one on sax, one on drums, one on piano, and one on an upright bass. They sounded just like Oscar Peterson's quartet. There were five or six well-dressed burly white men in the club, and some ladies of the evening out in the day. I wanted to grab one of the musicians by the hand and get to doing some swing to that fine jazz, but I hadn't come there for any of that. Or for the drinking that they were all doing. Or any of the other shit they looked like they were about to get into with those women.

A man with a strong presence like Mr. Benjamin stood near a table in the middle of the action. This had to be Babe.

People came up to him and shook his hand. He was around six-four, with black wavy hair and olive skin. His strong physique was noticeable under his tailored gray suit, an outfit that said he was somebody. I felt a quiver in my body. His confident air was sexy. Today, whenever I see the actor Russell Crowe, I am reminded of Babe and his rugged but suave presence.

A deliveryman standing beside him pulled a pen from behind his ear so Babe could sign some paperwork. I focused myself and sauntered right over to him. None of the men or women in the joint had noticed me until that point. I wore an emerald-green trench coat tied at the waist with my hair pressed and crimped just a little where it was parted. My makeup and the fine necklace, earrings, black leather handbag, and black leather shoes said that I was somebody too.

I shook his hand. "My name is Doris Payne. I'd like to have a word with you. Ada Lurch sent me your way." I made sure that my tone was as clear as a precious diamond, and he knew I wasn't there for any of that showgirl shit. I was there as a woman on his level. He smiled—a broad smile I would see many more times, a smile that said, *Whatever you say, Doris*—and he pulled out a chair.

It was a straightforward business proposition. I needed a third of the price tag. If he got more than the agreed-upon selling price, that was his. I showed him my Montreal piece.

"That is gorgeous. You got this?" he asked.

I projected my confidence instead of my infatuation. "If you end up my buyer, don't question me. I wouldn't have come to you if I wasn't capable."

He was impressed. It was a deal. I wouldn't work for him, and he wouldn't work for me.

In one of our first conversations, I told Babe how I did what I did.

He didn't believe me. He said, "Hon, there must be more to it. My brothers are not that stupid."

"Yes, they are. You have to see it." I defended the truth and my hard work. I hadn't just come into it at twenty-seven years old thinking I was slick. I had practiced. I knew if I did it right, I could get a whole lot of money. "Preparation is the biggest thing," I told him. It didn't take much time for him to decide he wanted to see it happen.

THE NEXT DAY I got up early and admired myself in the bathroom mirror of my new house. I didn't have to share the bathroom with the kids that day because half the time they were with their father back in West Virginia. I sat at my vanity taking a smoke before dawn. If I could pull this off, it wouldn't be just about proving myself to Babe. I could start buying the kids more of the things they wanted, like dance lessons for Rhonda and sleepaway camp for Ronny. I flipped through the latest copy of *Charm* to the page I had folded down, showing a diamond worn by a manicured white hand stretched out over a cherrywood background. Babe had said he knew a place that would have a piece like this, a new jewelry store in Philadelphia. "I'll take you there, but I'll also call a few folks who can get you out on bond because, hon, we're about to find out that my brothers are not that stupid."

THERE I WAS again in a black Fleetwood, but this one Babe owned. We were like two kids taking off on a dare adventure, dressed up in our finest. We looked like some rich, famous couple out for a late-fall vacation. The sky was thick with gray clouds that looked like they were about to drop a ton of snow. All the way there, Babe teased me. "I'm telling you, this guy knows all the men in sports and knows a thing or two. You better watch yourself. You can't put one past him."

I told him about my Montreal campaign. "I'm slick as silk. You'll see."

We got a room together at a hotel. The next day I put on my fine brown suit, my jewels, and my green trench coat, and went to work. Snow was just beginning to fall when we parked. I didn't want to admit it, but there was something very movie-star romantic about it all.

The jewelry store was in the historic LeGar Building downtown. I walked in first and then Babe followed a few moments later. I was a little shocked at how small it was. It was just a little U-shaped family-owned place. At least Babe had enough sense to carry on a conversation about sports and shit with the owner while I worked with one of the clerks. That was the other problem: the store clerk was a woman. I wasn't going to charm her so easily. I had worn my fine wedding set so I would appear married but alone shopping that day.

I told my clerk, "I am interested in a round diamond, two and a half carats, maybe more." I was in there about forty minutes because it took some doing to find a common conversation with this woman. Turned out, she was into my outfit. I got her rambling about the fashions for working women, and after a while, she finally confused herself and showed me an assortment of fine pieces while talking and not looking down. Among the pieces I shuffled around was the ring I wanted. It was a clear emerald-cut diamond. The four Cs that determine a diamond's value are color, clarity, cut, and carat weight. If a diamond has lots of cuts, it has lots of sparkle, but cuts are sometimes made to remove imperfections in the clarity, like specks, tiny holes, and fractures. The more you cut away, the fewer the carats, or actual weight, of the diamond. Anything more than two carats that is clear and colorless is rare and of high value. I had come a long way from not knowing the difference between an emerald-cut diamond and something from a Cracker Jack box.

Once it was on my finger, intuitively Babe set up a distraction. He asked the owner about his daughter. The shop owner waved to his daughter, who was serving me. "Come here, and let me introduce you to a real live college MVP."

She left me looking at the ring, and I casually walked out of the store.

I got myself a cab and went to another hotel first, just in case I was being followed. Then, at two o'clock, an hour after I had taken the piece, I rendezvoused with Babe at our hotel. We only had to meet up to leave, no need to celebrate or anything. Our bags were already packed. I followed him in whatever direction he walked, toward the bathroom, then out the front door, where, lucky for us, the snow was really starting to come down. The valet pulled the Fleetwood around, again bowing as if I was some rich movie star and Babe was my rich husband. We were off, headed up the highway back to Cleveland.

Babe was as loud talking about it all as I was.

"I can't believe it," he said. That was the first time I heard his laugh, coming from somewhere deep in his firm gut.

I laughed too. "I told you."

It was snowing so hard. The radio blared, and we laughed about the image of us stuck on the highway, a Black woman and a white man in a Fleetwood knee-deep in snow. We then got quiet so Babe could concentrate and see where he was going. The windshield wipers made a swooshing sound. An old Count Basie tune came on. Babe called himself trying to hit on me, singing, *"Take me back, baby, you're all I'm craving for."* With one hand on the wheel, he walked his fingers across the seat and put his hand in mine. I wasn't the blushing type, but he had me with that. I sang back, and held his hand, *"Take me back, Babe, you're all I'm craving for."* His large muscular hand around my small hand felt safe and sensual.

We got to laughing all over again, mostly because neither

of us could sing. Then the music stopped, and it popped up on the car radio: "Breaking news: An interracial couple entered a jewelry salon in Philadelphia and stole a valuable jewel."

Babe acted like a girl having her first period. We swerved in the snow. He had to take his hands and feet off everything to get the car back under control. Just like that, he went from high and happy to panic-stricken. The idea of being stopped on the highway for robbery was not his idea of being a good Jew boy, and on top of it, being mixed up in a robbery with a Black woman. I tried to calm him by singing to him. "*Take me back, baby, you're all I'm craving for.*" I thought it was funny. He didn't. It was exciting and racy to me to be in this situation with him.

He dropped me off at my place that night and he went to his. I had done what needed to be done. Babe had the piece. Now it was all in his hands to sell it and give me my third. I trusted he could do what he said, just like I had shown him I could do what I said. That night I rested easy.

The next morning, I got up and had breakfast with my mom. The two of us read the paper before she went off to work. I could tell she wanted to ask me where I had been off to, but we were long past those types of questions of each other. Shoot, I had suspected for a long time that she had been seeing someone when she had left Daddy to do seamstress work, but the two of us kept each other's peace.

Late that night, Babe called. As it turned out, he hadn't

gone to bed at all the night before. Instead, he'd stayed up making calls and arranging things with his connections because he felt like he couldn't move the piece without me going to jail. He said, "Hon, they described you to a T. I've talked with the DA in Philly. They're going to come and pick you up if you don't self-surrender."

This is the end? I haven't even gotten started. I didn't want to just go marching myself into a jail cell. What was I going to tell my kids? "Why in the world would I go turn myself in? Why did you go calling the DA? You just should have sold the piece and kept your damned mouth shut."

He tried interrupting me, but I got it all out. When I'd had my say, he spoke up. "Hon, listen. I know the DA and the judge too. We have worked some things together in the past. It's a formality. You'll go, satisfy the police. You won't take the ring with you. You won't say a word. The DA and the judge have it all arranged. You will self-surrender but will come on back home, and that will be that. A lawyer is going to meet you at the precinct. Just trust me."

I swallowed hard and imagined my mother getting a phone call that I was locked up in Philly. I calculated the possibility of running, but there were the kids to consider. And I didn't run from anybody. It was just something I refused to do. I sighed into the phone.

Babe quieted his voice, trying to reassure me. "I'll come and get you and take you to the airport. You'll be back before evening."

I got dressed, thinking this was either the dumbest thing

I'd ever done or I was lucky I'd met Babe when I did. I found out soon enough.

I FLEW OUT. I got a cab to the Philadelphia precinct Babe instructed me to go to. When I got out of the cab, it was raining, and I must have looked like a scared little girl sitting there. I had never been fingerprinted, had never been in a damned jail. A lanky older Italian man, the attorney Babe had described, stood there under an umbrella. "Miss Payne?" His voice was gravelly, and he reached the umbrella out to escort me into the police station. I got fingerprinted, photographed, "self-surrendered" for theft, but I wasn't questioned, nobody even asked me about the ring. It was a revolving door. In and out. I kept waiting for somebody to come chase after me as the attorney walked with me to get into a cab, but off I went, back to the airport.

Babe met my flight in Cleveland. "See? Easy as pie." He dropped me off at home as if it was all in a day's work. "This is just part of it, hon. If you're going to deal in moving big gems, you're going to have the business of going down and satisfying the judge with a confession of guilt, then having your money connections post bail while a well-connected lawyer handles the rest. The bail is part of the cost of doing business."

He was right. Nobody at the police station had asked me for the ring. Babe, the lawyer, the DA, the judge, and likely the police chief were all in cahoots, owing each other one favor or another. Babe still had the diamond and lay low with it for another week before he sold it to a buyer. I got my cut and he got his.

I sent the kids' father a big-ass check, and he was on to me. He wasn't a bad dude, but he found out through the grapevine what I was doing for a living and said the kids needed to stay with him full-time and that I needed to pay child support. Babe advised me to go see a judge in Cleveland. The judge said that having a criminal record didn't make me an unfit mother. He told me I just needed to financially provide for my children and have a stable home for them with the routines of an everyday life. I had the financial part covered, but a woman practicing being a world-class jewel thief wasn't going to be home much. I set out to offer the kids at least the financial stability I had always wanted as a child. I sent them to live with their father.

WHOM I MET through Babe and what I learned from him would prove to be the most valuable assets of my career. We had learned our lesson of being seen together in a store, that's for sure. We found other ways of helping each other. One weekend I went to Milwaukee, spent the night, woke up, and looked at magazines advertising the fine-jewelry stores there. I decided which one I would go to. Around noon, I went for a walk. While lying in bed in Cleveland,

Babe called the store, acting as my lawyer. He told the jeweler that I had come into some money and he had suggested I invest in fine jewels. The fella listened to Babe's voice and assumed he was a monied white man. He never asked for more information. The guy brought out more pieces. Babe said he got so tickled that he could hardly keep from laughing through the phone. We let their racial prejudice be the tool that made them con themselves.

BABE WAS MARRIED, which was fine with me. Even though our relationship eventually included sex, I wasn't down for any domestic shit. Like the women in Slab Fork who had "interesting" relationships, Myra, his wife, knew about Babe and me. She thought I was the nicest girl Babe had ever had. She came from money and was a good person to talk with about fashion. She once talked me into buying a mink coat from Cikra Furs of Cleveland. That's how social we were with each other. Two women who had different needs from one man.

Romance and domestic life was for Babe and Myra; sex and business was for Babe and me. It wasn't syrupy sweet, but we were as tight as two people could get. Every morning after Mom was off to her seamstress job, he came over my house, which became our playhouse. After some bedroom time, we sat in the kitchen with some smokes and coffee, and I discussed with him every aspect of any heist I was going to do.

"I'm planning on heading to Akron this weekend to get a piece."

He had the brains to shore up any of my plans to make sure neither of us got caught. "Don't even go in the place without stopping at a pay phone to call. I'll plan to call the store two or three times asking one question and another. That will keep at least one clerk busy while you do your thing."

The two of us could seriously cook up some shit with me having the nerve and him having the calculations and connections.

At noon, we'd get tight one more time, and he'd head back to the city to open up his nightclub at one o'clock. Those were our days, never any nighttime activity unless we were out of town or out on the town. A man wasn't going to sleep at my house, not even Babe. My home was our playhouse by day and a safe haven for me and Mom at night.

CHAPTER 11

RACIAL BACKFIRE

THE FIRST TIME I FLEW CROSS-COUNTRY, Babe took me to Vegas to see the Rat Pack: Dean Martin, Frank Sinatra, Sammy Davis Jr., Peter Lawford, and Joey Bishop all on stage for one show of clowning around. I was so excited I couldn't handle myself. "All in one show?"

"You'll see, they are going to have you laughing the whole time, hon."

We flew first class. That was the first time I'd experienced being on a plane with enough leg room to put my feet up if I wanted to. You should have seen the eyes peeking through the curtain from coach trying to figure us out, a refined-looking Black woman and a burly handsome Jew, laughing and flirting transcontinental style.

The Sands Hotel wasn't all drapery and chandeliers. It

was modern 1960s Googie-style architecture with sharp angles. The rooms had that look of the interior of a *Star Trek* vessel with boomerang-shaped tables and swivel bucket chairs. I preferred less modern and more elegant myself.

They sure didn't worry about the electric bill in Vegas—at night if it didn't light up, it wasn't worth looking at. The show was right there in the hotel. You should have seen how handsome Babe was in his black evening suit. He looked better than Dean Martin himself. On his arm, I wore a peach-colored evening gown, low cut with spaghetti straps, and a slit up the side that went damn near up to my waist. It had more sequins on it than there was fabric. Wrapped around my shoulders was a pink satin shawl. Vegas was the only place I could ever wear some shit that gaudy. Babe was grinning ear to ear, like I was his prize and he couldn't wait to show me off.

We laughed so hard at those five dudes acting out on stage. Dean Martin carried little Sammy Davis Jr. under his arm and walked off the stage thanking the NAACP for his award. They made it hard to maintain an air of class. Everybody was doubled over in stitches even though their jewels sparkled as much as the lights around us. I didn't miss the reality of the carat count in the audience even in the midst of the fun.

On the way home, I was like a kid who had just visited the world's largest candy store. I told Babe, "I've got to go back there. All that sparkle. Can you imagine what I can do?" We knew better than to talk the details of our work in public, but I kept that shit coded: "I can let the crow fly in, play with sparkly objects, and go back to my nest."

Babe smiled and patted my hand as he reclined his seat for the long flight. "Vegas stands alone. You can't get to any place else easily from there. It's too isolated." He then reminded me of the stronghold the mob had over that city. "It's also too overrun with other crows who have claimed those nests." He was a dyed-in-the-wool strategist and dropped a bit of knowledge for what he knew I was scheming. "Now, Los Angeles is where that crow can find plenty of space to fly with sparkly little toys all around her as far as the eye can see."

That's one of the strategies Babe taught me—go someplace where you can set up temporary home and operate from one location while taking from other nearby locations. If possible, be one of the only games in town. I carried that with me for the rest of my career.

IN THE 1960S, it was a lot of fun being in Los Angeles on my own, experiencing the free, open, and expressive social life. I could meet up with some folks, smoke some weed, go hear Etta James or Marvin Gaye. Many an afternoon I got dressed to the nines with dainty daytime diamonds and a pair of Louis Vuitton sunglasses. I sashayed down Sunset Boulevard just to watch people do that thing of pulling their sunglasses down and taking a long pause, trying to figure who this possibly famous woman was.

Everybody came through LA. Just a block away from what soon became my usual extended-stay motel, Sam Cooke was killed. I stood on the motel balcony that night watching the police come and go, first thinking they were looking for me and then hearing the news about him getting shot after reportedly trying to rape a woman.

I came and went from my motel as if it was my home away from home. I would go to Beverly Hills, straight to Rodeo Drive, and make a move—nothing special, my usual. I once made off with a couple of diamond rings worth a total of around $20,000, an amount of $162,000 today.

In August 1965, I went to Pasadena, to B. D. Howes and Son jewelers, and got a real cute ring worth around $4,000 ($32,000 in today's market), and I got away clean. My motel was a great little crow's nest. I could go out to anywhere high end, get something shiny, and bring it back.

If it was some piece of junk that was less than two carats, or showing small surface inclusions, I'd sell it in a club or something. People on the street didn't know a valuable diamond from one with flaws. If it was a true screamer, Babe would fly out to California, and we would meet up for what is now called a high-class "booty call" and some entertainment. I'd send him back to Cleveland with my loot. After selling it, his job was to put my third in my bank account, and when he came for the next pickup, bring me a big-ass lump of cash so I could keep on doing business in California, "cash on the barrelhead" style. For almost ten years of doing business with Babe, that's how I saw him and other Jews handle their dealings behind the scenes.

One time, Babe and I rendezvoused for the jewelry swap in San Francisco. We met up at the extravagant Inter-Continental Mark Hopkins Hotel. We lay around in the hotel room, and I decided to go to the Top of the Mark restaurant and see the views of the Bay Bridge and the San Francisco skyline. I wasn't so sure of going up there as a Black woman, no matter how well dressed. Babe was tired and said, "Hon, go on and get yourself a seat. You have enough going for you. The maître d' will take one look at you and take care of you."

I got dressed up and went up to dine alone. The maître d' came to my table and told me that a gentleman wanted me to dine with him. I didn't know it at the time, but it was the financial minister of Mali. We had a great conversation and an enjoyable meal. Afterward, he wanted my phone number. I gave him my mother's number. She got in touch with me and said, "A man called for you from your hotel."

I took his information and the next day I went and picked him up. We had a good social evening. I told Babe all about it, thinking he might be a little jealous, but he jumped straight to money thoughts. "Hon, there's a lot of money right there. Mali is a standout nation in the mining of gold and diamonds."

"Babe, I don't need you educating me about Africa, and the biggest mistake for you to make would be to tell me to make a play for his money. I might end up making a play for him."

He thought about that. "Well, since you brought it up, you may be right." We laughed about it, but I was serious even though I could tell the thought of me making it with another man made him nervous.

Babe asked me to fly back with him, and I reminded him that I wasn't done working in California, and his job was to get back to his connections and sell the fruits of my labor. I didn't think so much about what I was doing at the time, but looking back, I know I was testing to see if he had that jealousy bug that my father had. I also wanted him to know that I was not to be singled out as if I was his and only his. This wasn't some mistress shit. I was a free agent with work to do.

THAT SUMMER, all hell broke loose in Watts, one of the urban sections of Los Angeles. A young Black man, who was on parole for robbery, got stopped and a fight broke out with police, who went nuts, calling more and more police to an already hot situation. More than a thousand people were injured, a thousand buildings were burned, and thirty-four people died—all but a few of them Black. That whole region of the city was a war zone for six days, and the police in the whole LA area were jumpy as hell.

One November night in 1965, I got a call from my son, Ronald, who had finished his army basic training and was stationed in Amberg, Germany. "Mom, I believe you're in *Jet* magazine. Not you, but I think they mean you." He was looking out for me all the way from Germany.

I got the magazine. There was an article about a theft I

had committed in Pasadena. The headline read "Margherite Mays Cleared in $4,000 California Gem Theft."

They thought she stole a piece in Pasadena from B. D. Howes and Son jewelers. I remembered that job—it was a beautiful piece of ice, a three-carat solitaire, in a platinum setting, the gem elevated like Kilimanjaro to show its cuts and brilliance.

Except Margherite Wendell Chapman was the suspect. She was now divorced from the famous San Francisco Giants baseball player Willie Mays.

Every time I walked into a store in my expensive duds and jewelry, they thought I was someone famous they couldn't quite place. This was the first time someone famous was being mistaken for me. They thought a famous Black woman had been getting away with jewel theft. I didn't have notoriety for what I had been doing, but this was evidence that someone had established my pattern. *I've blown some shit now.* I knew what I was doing, why I was doing it. But I wasn't trying to get another sister caught in the middle of my shit. Judge Fletcher dismissed the charges, but word was, they were searching for the nigger who really took the shit.

MY EXTENDED-STAY MOTEL was near the Los Angeles airport just in case I needed to get the hell out of there, but I didn't get my shit packed fast enough. The police banged on the door. "Doris Payne!" Somehow they'd tracked me to that motel even though I didn't go telling folks where I was.

They detained me even though they didn't have anything specific they were detaining me for. Babe had long sold that piece into the Cleveland black market. I made my phone call to Babe and told him what was happening. He got emotional and told me, "Hang in there. I'm going to set you up with Richard Caballero." He was a Los Angeles lawyer with East Coast ties who had dealt with these types of incidents. Attorney Caballero came to see me that night and let me know that the police didn't have anything on me. We were both pretty sure they were detaining me in an attempt to clear up the Margherite Wendell Chapman accusation. They had to find the well-to-do Black woman who had committed the actual robbery. Chapman had a solid alibi and wasn't going to get stuck with my crime. Nor was I, because even though I had done it, there was no evidence.

I fell silent that night. The worst thing in the world for me would be prison. I couldn't do it. I knew I couldn't. They took me to Sybil Brand Institute for Women, which was cushy for a prison. It was a cross between a women's prison and a college campus. It even had a small hospital and activities like cooking and sewing to keep the inmates busy. I told myself, *This is Girl Scouts. You can deal with this.*

After a few days, officers from Pasadena came and transported me from Sybil Brand in LA County to a Pasadena jail. I immediately called Caballero, who was in Beverly Hills, to let him know what was happening. He was in court, but I told his secretary that it was an emergency. I didn't know what they were going to do to me, and I felt it was regarding the Margherite Wendell Chapman situation. Caballero called me back and said, "Don't open your mouth."

About twenty minutes later, they took me back to Sybil Brand. The next morning they released me on bail. I took a flight back to Cleveland that had a layover in Phoenix, Arizona. There the FBI arrested me. They allowed me to make a call to let my family know where I was, and I called Babe. He didn't get downright mad often, but he blurted out, "The FBI? They don't have a case with you. Fuck this!"

A few minutes later, I heard an announcement in the airport: "Miss Doris Payne, please go to the nearest courtesy phone and pick up." The FBI agents escorted me to one of the phones. It was one of Babe's contacts. He told me the name of a bail bondsman to call once they took me back to LA. I followed his instructions and held on to the bail bondsman's name. The same bail bondsman in later years would work with Angela Davis.

After I was released on bail, I went back to my motel because I was not allowed to leave the state until the hearing. I about chewed my nails clean down to nubs not knowing what was going to happen next. Caballero got the case moved from downtown LA to Beverly Hills, and all of a sudden the worst thing for my career happened. I was bigtime.

When we got to court, media cameras were everywhere. So many pictures were snapped of me from every angle. Everybody wanted to see the woman who passed for the rich Black socialite Margherite Wendell Chapman. I knew my face would now be recognizable all over the country. My job from then on would be much more challenging, but I always knew how to think myself out of a pinch.

Meanwhile, Margherite Wendell Chapman's attorney mentioned a lawsuit for damages resulting from allegations against her client. My lawyer told me to keep quiet, that this could play in our favor, because the courts were already in the middle of so much attention for accusing a Black woman who lived in New York, who was the ex-wife of a famous baseball player, and who managed the careers of entertainers like Gladys Knight. They had randomly accused a good-looking well-dressed Black woman of stealing jewels when they had no evidence. Sitting in the hallway, awaiting the judge's decision about me, I listened to the FBI agent who had detained me talk to a reporter as if I weren't present.

"Nobody has ever caught her with a piece, but at this point we know she's been doing this for at least a decade."

The reporter just said, "Uh-huh."

Caballero later said the reporters had likely been paid off by the City of Pasadena to keep their pens quiet. The city wouldn't want the publicity for trying to fix the situation by simply arresting yet another Black woman without evidence when all around the nation and right there in LA there was so much racial tension.

The judge called us all back into his chambers, and they let me off.

Pasadena gave me a prison number, issued through their system, even though I wasn't convicted. I believe this was to please the Pasadena judicial system. On paper, it looked as if I had served time for stealing the ring. In reality, I went on with my life. Fine-jewelry stores didn't want the world to know how a Black woman was stealing gems from right under their noses.

It would have soothed their egos if they could have blamed it on the charms of someone like Margherite Wendell Chapman or Lena Horne. They didn't want to believe a Black coal miner's daughter was walking into their stores and walking out with their livelihoods.

That prison number without prison time would come back to bite me thirty-some years later. My notoriety and face recognition in the media would also come back to haunt me. How was I going to be the sly fox I had always been if people knew what I looked like?

CHAPTER 12

IT'S WHO YOU KNOW, BUT YOU DON'T OWN ME

N THE SUMMER OF 1966, RACE RIOTS BROKE OUT all over the City of Cleveland. The Hough neighborhood, where we lived, saw some of the worst tension. Few Blacks owned homes. Most of them rented from white landlords who had fled the neighborhoods in the 1950s and taken their grocery stores and good schools with them. I knew I didn't want to remain living in the part of town that saw the worst of it.

I drove around the Shaker Heights neighborhood, a suburb of Cleveland. When I was there, I felt myself exhale from the tension and close quarters of the houses in the Hough neighborhood. Every house in Shaker Heights had a driveway. All of them were two stories. And the streets were tree-lined and peaceful. I would be one of the Black people to break through the color line in that part of town. I felt comfortable there, like the neighborhood was fitting for the status I had attained.

One day I cruised down Scottsdale Boulevard and saw a FOR SALE sign on a house I fell in love with. It was a Tudor-style home, made of brick and stucco with stone archways. I just sat there in my fancy car, feeling like I was in an English storybook.

The realtor met me at the house the next day. He was a round, squat, red-haired fellow. He stood on the lawn and peeked and peeked as I pulled into the driveway. He didn't hide that he was curious about who was driving up in a car like mine. I could see his face light up, though, happy about the commission. When I stepped out, it didn't seem to bother him at all that I was a Black woman. He just saw dollar signs.

I wore a beige suit and a tiny fox fur I had purchased in admiration of Ada Lurch's style. He shook my hand too vigorously and hopped up the stone steps, like a man who had just won the lottery. The wood floors and wood pillars inside were just what I had expected. It was so upscale that you couldn't have flowers in the front yard without the approval of the homeowners' association. They had more restrictions than a pimp had for a hooker, but I wanted that house. I was home.

All I had to do was figure out how I was going to get a loan for a four-bedroom, $20,000 brick house. In the 1960s, that was equivalent to a $250,000 house now. I had half that amount in the bank but didn't want to go around advertising on some loan application where a Black woman got that sort of money.

Babe saw it differently. He believed that we cry about so many things and put it on race rather than just figure out how things are done. That was hard to swallow considering everything happening around us in Cleveland and the nation at that time. What I took from his words was that I could complain about the state of things in the country and want a house in Shaker Heights, or I could use the intelligence that had always served me well and figure out how to get that house.

Babe reminded me that he had sold some of my pieces to bank presidents. So off we went to see Mr. Morrie Nidus. He was the president of my bank. He had never met me, but when he saw me with Babe, he knew who I was. I told him about the house I wanted to purchase and where it was located. He didn't ask about my credit. He asked, "What do you currently net yearly on the jewelry you sell?"

I looked at Babe because I was thinking this was some kind of setup. Babe nodded ever so gently. I said with my head up, "Around fifty thousand dollars."

He got up from the desk.

I whispered to Babe, "What the hell?"

He tapped my shoulder and whispered back, "It's fine. It's fine."

Mr. Nidus came back and said some *Mission: Impossible*–sounding shit. "The phone will ring. Just answer it." The three of us sat there, and sure enough, the phone rang. It was a loan officer, who simply asked me my name and that was that. I ended up with a loan. The house in Shaker Heights was all mine.

I DIDN'T LIKE it one bit when Babe started bringing potential buyers to my new house. "You don't have that kind of clout in my life to take center stage like that." I was so upset with him. It wasn't uncommon for somebody white to come to a house in Shaker Heights, but I didn't want folks who were buying from me to be in my home. It was too much like shitting where you eat.

Again, he reminded me that if a person had any political status and was interested in buying a piece, they had to come see me. According to him, these people were my freedom. I wouldn't have to worry about the police locally if I was selling to them and everybody they were in cahoots with. I calmed down a bit. Babe's income was tied to my actions. He wasn't going to do anything to get too far on my bad side. He sometimes got $12,000 or $13,000 from me stealing one piece. If a fencer was earning that today, he'd be netting $100,000 on each piece. People took one glance at someone who looked like an upstanding, well-dressed Jewish man and bought from him much faster than if they saw the Black woman behind it all.

SOME OF MY most consistent buyers were the Lonardo brothers. They were Cleveland mafia who had their hands in the city's money, everything from bail bonds to bars and clubs. People didn't know that Frank and Dominic orchestrated their movements and that they lived on a tab connected to these two. Babe often sold the wedding sets I stole to the Lonardo family for a wedding that was soon to come. For a long time they had known my name, but they hadn't ever seen me, because Babe was the seller. I didn't mind being connected to them via Babe's sales, but honestly, they made me nervous. I didn't like unpredictable shit.

That all changed one day when Babe needed to meet Frank Lonardo at the bail bondsman's office to pick up the cash from a sale Babe had entrusted to Frank. I didn't like the idea of a second party moving goods, so I came along to protect my own interest.

I dressed upscale, the way I always did. Babe and I walked in. He and a tall, square-faced, dark-haired man shook hands. In Frank's mind, he was selling the piece for Babe. He handed Babe the envelope and ignored that I was standing there. Frank spoke with authority, as if he was in charge of the transaction. "Here's most of it. I'm going to hold on to ten thousand dollars if you're fine with that."

Babe thumbed through the contents of the envelope and said back, "Don't ask me, ask Doris," motioning with the envelope toward me.

Frank stretched his neck up out of his collar and pulled on his suit lapel the way jewelry clerks did when they were trying to get ahold of their thoughts. His furrowed brow told me that this situation didn't sit too well with him.

I stared him in the eyes. "It's okay with me."

Frank turned back to Babe. "You want me to do business with this nigger bitch?"

The next thing, the envelope hit the floor and Babe sucker punched the second-most-noted mafia boss in Cleveland, the first being Frank's older brother, Dominic. The clerk behind the window at the end of the hall disappeared as if we were in some old western and a gunfighter had entered.

Babe stood there with his fists ready, which wouldn't have done much good if Frank had pulled a gun on him. For several seconds Frank held his jaw, and Babe held his dukes up. They didn't say anything. Babe still had the body of the MVP football player he had once been. Any man going toe to toe with him would have to calculate the force of a freight train behind his punch. Frank turned and walked out the door. Babe picked the money up off the floor. He tried to hide that he was shaking, and we got the hell out of there.

"Hon, I think I'll put Myra up in a hotel and come stay with you until things cool down."

I told him without hesitation, "No, you won't. Punching Frank was what you should have done, but that don't set you a place in my bed."

He combed his fingers through his wavy hair the way he did when he was irritated with me. "You're kidding, right? Frank might come for you like he might come after me?"

He didn't like it when I laughed at comments like that, but we stood there in the parking lot of the bail bondsman's office, me smirking and him running his fingers through his hair.

"You sure can be hard on a man, hon."

I DIDN'T HEAR from Babe for a few days. I called Myra, who said, "He hasn't been home in two nights. I thought he was with you." Babe had gone underground in fear of retaliation from the Lonardos.

The next Monday, I got dressed and drove myself to the Murray Hill district, the Little Italy of Cleveland. I had that fox fur around my shoulders, diamond teardrop earrings on, and walked right into Dominic Lonardo's bar. I knew that Frank's reputation was at stake if his brother knew he owed money to a woman and was refusing to pay. Nigger or no nigger, Italian men didn't believe in that kind of cowardice.

Dominic stepped away from paperwork in his office and listened as I told the shortened story without details. He got up. "Stay put for a minute." I heard the muffled sounds of him and Frank arguing. Dominic came back into the office with an envelope with my money in it. I didn't say thank you or any kind of shuffling thing. I just nodded and left, all gangster-like. Shit, I walked in there as Doris Payne, but I walked out all Pam Grier and Foxy Brown. *Nobody was going to fuck with my money.*

Frank had to face that I was the one who was in charge

of the money, not Babe. After that day, the Lonardo brothers and I were like family. We sat down over many meals together. If I ever needed to get out of a pinch, they fixed it.

I HAD ACCEPTED the racial imbalance in my life because of what I was able to do with it, but my relationship with Mr. Benjamin had taught me that racial imbalance couldn't exist in a close relationship.

When Babe and I went out, we didn't go to the Black side of Cleveland, where I wanted to hang. We went to a jazz place in Manhattan that Johnny Carson's nephew owned. I think Babe liked other white men to see him with a pretty, light-skinned, high-class Black woman on his arm. I was his Lena Horne and he was my Lennie Hayton.

We had little spats about constantly flying to San Francisco or Manhattan to go out. I loved being at fine hotels, like the Ritz, fine clubs that celebrities frequented. But with all of the racial tension in Cleveland between whites and Blacks, sometimes I just wanted to be in a speakeasy with a bunch of other Black people, laughing or acting crazy about what was happening in the streets. Most folks didn't even know that the term "speakeasy" came from my West Virginia coal-mine upbringing.

On Saturday night after payday, my daddy would get together with some of the other Black coal miners, and just like the women would go to one house to get their hair done, the men would go to one house to get to playing cards and hollering and having a good time with any of the women who weren't churchgoers. The music would be so loud you could hear it thumping in the night on our little Slab Fork Road. It was the release they needed after a hellish workweek.

The constable couldn't go arresting all of the town's workers for being noisy, so instead the rule was that a Black Saturday-night house party had to cover its windows so the lights didn't bother other people. And after a certain hour, they had to play the music low and "speak easy"—whisper rather than keep the rest of the town awake all night.

BABE WARNED, "HOW CAN I protect you if you're hanging out on the shady side of town?" He showed me how to make a weapon out of a single-edge razor blade. He told me, "The best thing a woman alone can have is this." He took some tape and wrapped it around the end of the blade and said, "See? You can carry it, and you should never go to your car without it." He demonstrated, holding it to his own neck. "You know they're going to get you around the neck, so get them in the eyes with it."

I told him, "I'm not engaging in any brutal shit like that."

"Hon, it's you or them."

Babe knew the robberies on the Black side of town were prominent, and I appreciated him caring, but I never had to use that blade, though I kept it in my purse just in case.

Babe said, "I can spend more time at your house."

My answer was simple: "No." I had the new house, the kids were living full-time with their dad, and my mother was dating a guy and had gotten her own place. Things were lonely whenever he and I weren't in the middle of our morning sex and work routine, but I still didn't want any man living in my house, trying to control me.

CHAPTER 13

FAMILY TIES AND KNOWN ASSOCIATES

SHIRLEY SOLD FINE DESIGNER SPORTSWEAR at the May Company department store. I would walk in and take the elevator to her floor, even though I didn't wear those fashions. She was very attractive. She had dark, pretty hair and was petite like me. We had a lot in common. We wore the same size, were about the same age, and both had had difficult upbringings.

One of our favorite funny things to say if one of us saw the other all dressed up was "Ooo. You ain't no government bum."

Shirley worked in the department store on weekdays and was a barmaid at different bars on the weekends, including the Winston Speakeasy, an after-hours club. The two jobs helped her pay for her mother's house. We had that in common too. "No matter what, take care of your mom."

Her mom—or actually, the woman who had raised her—was a prostitute who found Shirley under a tree in Delight, Arkansas. This woman was so popular as a high-end prostitute that she had met Marvin Gaye and introduced Shirley to him once. She had made sure Shirley had a good upbringing despite her profession.

When Shirley's mother died, the house went to the woman's son, who was a pimp in New York. Thanks to the woman who had raised her, Shirley had good enough manners and qualities to not go kill somebody over that. Even though she said she was wounded by not getting part of the house, she spoke highly of her mother.

We both had been through some shit and had come out of it on our own. We both were women who knew how to take care of ourselves. Though Shirley worked at bars at night, neither one of us drank. When I was younger, I had seen a woman vomiting, and my mom had said, "She's been drinking liquor."

"I'm never going to do that," I said. I didn't want anything interfering with my ability to take care of my mom and my kids.

Shirley was such a hardworking woman, but we managed to hang out and keep up with each other's lives. After her mother died, she didn't have anybody. She didn't have any kids, but she had me, and she knew what a friend meant. She had my back and I had hers.

One day the police came to my house, looking for me and Babe. Shirley was in the kitchen fixing a meal. I wasn't home. They arrested her, thinking she was me. They didn't ask for her name, ID, or anything. They just called "Doris Payne" and arrested her. She didn't try to tell them who she really was. She let them believe what they wanted until things could be cleared up.

Babe self-surrendered from home about eight hours after Shirley got arrested. I found out and went downtown at ten a.m., during court time. That's when they found out they had the wrong light-skinned, petite Black woman. Babe had lawyers to meet us there, and everything was straightened out behind the scenes. Shirley had my back and Babe's back, and became part of our family.

I DIDN'T HANG out as much as I wanted to. I would go down to my mom's to hang and play bid whist or something until midnight, then to the Winston Speakeasy or whatever bar Shirley was working so we could hang out.

One night I was with Shirley at one of her other jobs, and she said, "What you having, darling?" I bought drinks and gave them away to men so she'd get some good tips from dudes who thought some hot woman was interested. I quoted the song "One Bourbon, One Scotch, One Beer." We laughed real good.

She came out from behind the bar with the drinks on a tray. "I know exactly who you're buying these for tonight. I want you to meet this fella."

She brought me to the table of a tall man who looked like the boxing promoter Don King. He introduced himself as Kenneth Tolliver. "This," she said, nodding toward me as she placed the drinks on the table for him and his two flunky-looking friends, "this is one bad sistah, Doris Payne."

Kenneth was from Tennessee. We talked and got to laughing. I asked him about the jewelry he wore. He told me about the Piaget watch and pinkie ring with an emerald-cut diamond. The ring and the watch were beautiful and showed he had class. In our laughing and carrying on, he told me he was into selling drugs. That stopped me for a minute. He had been to prison and was educated with big words, though he had never been to school. "A Black brotha has the perfunctory position of supporting the wealth of white men who flaunt their treasures."

I said, "Nigga, what are you talkin' about?" We laughed our asses off.

He had street smarts and knew every shady thing about the shady side of Black Cleveland. He was best buddies with Muhammad Ali and every Black entertainer who breezed through town.

ONE NIGHT KENNETH and I were hanging out at the speakeasy. I had smoked enough weed to cure a ham. I was way too high to be driving myself back home. It was snowing and sleeting, so I had him drive my Fleetwood back to my house in Shaker Heights. I didn't want him or any other man sleeping at my house, so I let him keep my Fleetwood, knowing he would return it.

That night he was picked up by the Shaker Heights police, who used a law that had been on the books since zero hundred. The law said a convict couldn't be in the city of Shaker Heights for any reason. It was a law that made the white people of Shaker Heights feel false safety from the Black people in Cleveland. It had never been enforced.

There were riots happening in Cleveland, but the police in that area knew me, knew what I did for a living, and had respect for me. I didn't understand what the hell was happening until I thought it through. Nobody minded Babe coming and going from my house. Then I knew who'd had Kenneth picked up. Babe.

He said he didn't, but I knew he had orchestrated the whole mess through his connections. I had to go to court to testify that I knew Kenneth, but he got a trespassing charge on his record anyway.

The prosecutor, who also knew me and knew Babe, called me down to his office and told me that he had so much respect for me as a single Black woman who was capable of handling her business the way I was. He told me to stay away from the likes of Kenneth. He said, "You don't want to go getting mixed up with somebody like that." I sure as hell didn't need a father figure. This man was not going to help me, and I didn't have anybody else to get this one taken care of. Kenneth was just going to have to live with it.

✦

BABE WAS JEALOUS. That was something I was not going to deal with. I continued to go out of town to work. But
any day I was in town, I didn't want Babe to come to my
house for our usual time in the bed and time at the planning table. Instead, I dropped by to see Babe at his home. I
would stay and talk with Myra. She was a tall, good-looking,
olive-skinned Jewish woman who could have passed for a
model. I enjoyed her company. It wasn't like getting down
and having a conversation with Shirley about what was happening in the streets, but she was a woman who understood
fashion and fine things the way I did, and always had great
advice on purchases. "Before you buy any fur, remember
to pull the fur down to the roots to see if it is woven and
fake, or like your hair sprouting out of the scalp." She was
hands-on and down-to-earth even though her family had
money. Myra parted her black thick hair and said, "See,
look at that. Now look at this fur. Same thing." Then she
laughed at herself.

Half the time I was going over there testing out the possibility of staying Babe's business partner without the sex.
How would we all get along if I wasn't handling the sexual
reality in their relationship? I didn't admit it to myself that
his jealousy had turned me off, and I was looking to switch
it up.

Myra had a very rare illness that Babe said ran in the
pedigree of European Jews. All day she was normal and

worked at her job at an eyeglass maker. In the evening her system would run down like a clock. She didn't shake or anything, but by around five p.m. she couldn't even walk. I would be visiting her, and she would have to go get in bed, not even able to pick up something from the nightstand. I guess that ruined any possibility of a good sex life for them. At the time, only five cases of this illness were known to medical science, and she was one of them. It slowly progressed in her mom and her. Babe never talked much about her condition, but I saw it for myself.

Once Myra's system ran down for the evening, I would head out. Babe would always ask, "Where are you going? Want me to come over in the morning?"

"No, I'll stop by tomorrow evening."

Even if I wasn't going to be hanging out doing anything special, I had my mom and my friends Shirley and Kenneth. That was hard for Babe. After what happened to Kenneth, Babe and I continued to grow further apart, and he managed to find ways to draw me back to him.

He was very physique-conscious and convinced himself that taking off the weight he gained since I met him would bring us back together. He heard about the tummy tuck procedure. They could now perform it with almost no scarring. So he went to have one.

It was a one-day procedure. But his doctor, one of my associates, called and told me that Babe was having complications. He begged Babe to go to the Cleveland Clinic after the surgery, but Babe refused. "I don't need the people at the clinic commenting on my choices. I know half the administration." The doctor was concerned that he might have thrombosis, and he did.

He was going to be on blood thinners and doing his exercise and rest regiment for some time. I found myself using our time away from each other to think about ways I might want to go solo in the business. Even though Babe was sick, he still worried himself over what I was doing and whom I was doing it with. He would call, "Hey, hon, you alone?"

I kept reminding myself that he was married. He and Myra were each other's family, in sickness and in health. Even if I decided to start seeing Kenneth or someone else, that wasn't going to be his concern.

One day I was at home, making some dinner with Shirley, and the phone rang. I answered, "No, Babe, I'm not alone. Shirley's here. You want to talk to her?" Shirley and I laughed out into the kitchen.

It was Myra's voice that came through the phone, sounding weak and run-down. "Babe is gone."

My first thought was that he left her and called himself on his way to my house. "Don't worry, Myra. When he gets here, I'll turn him right back around."

She was just sucking in air now, like she was about to choke on something, "No, Doris, Babe died." I dropped the phone and the spiral cord let it hit the floor twice before Shirley picked it up, listened, and said, "Um-hm" over and over and hung up. She stared at me, like she was waiting for what she knew would come. I started crying so hard, I felt like I was drowning.

I didn't go to Babe's funeral. I didn't think it was the right thing for me to do. I went to the house during shiva. Shirley came with me, and the two of us just stayed quiet. There wasn't much in the way of tradition. No one sat in low chairs; there wasn't anybody in deep prayer. I looked from my one spot to another, refusing to walk around, which might mean remembering Babe. Myra came and hugged me long and hard, and I told myself not to cry, to let her cry, *Doris, don't cry.* I stayed on the sidelines of the living room and let his family members come to me. They knew who I was, knew I would respect the family.

I DIDN'T KNOW what to do with my feelings. I was overwhelmed by Babe's absence. Mornings were the hardest. I would spring up out of the bed. I didn't know a person could dream a sound, but I would hear Babe turn the key in the door, but when I went to the steps to look downstairs, I was there alone. It was then that I realized that Babe had been all I needed. Other than Shirley and my mom, I didn't connect with too many people.

With Babe gone, I could see the ways my upbringing had made it impossible for me to fully trust men, made it so I could never let them get too close. It had worked out perfectly that Babe was married, because I didn't want any of that domestic shit, but now he was gone, and I couldn't stop thinking how I wanted to wake up and for it to be a mistake. Maybe I should have gone to the funeral and seen him put into the ground. That was the hardest part. I wanted to go back in time and give him my heart, not just sex, but it was too late.

I had all those thoughts in my head as Babe's death settled down on me. I reminded myself I was doing the best I could. I would find somebody else white and in the business to buy my shit, but Babe had been so much more. He had been my protection, my silent partner, the man I could tighten it up with without being controlled, and the man who had helped me change my mind-set about a lot of the notions I had from childhood that had held me back. I hadn't wanted to admit that I loved him because I didn't operate much with that word. Mom taught me that love happened with somebody you cared about, who had your back and you had theirs, and that's what he had been to me.

PART III

CUT

A diamond's cut is its ability to interact with light—to give off sparkle and brilliance—and the cut is what enables the white light hitting a diamond to emit every color of the spectrum. The diamond cut grading consists of five ratings: Excellent, Very Good, Good, Fair, Poor. The cut is also the most difficult of the four *Cs* to determine, because of the many variables in the evaluation of the craftsmanship. Emerald, round, marquise, Asscher, pear, oval, heart—these are some of the cut shapes and varieties to be found in diamonds. A round brilliant cut, because of its many facets, will give off the most brilliance. Emerald cuts, or rectangular cuts, because of their elongation, will show more surface, and an emerald-cut diamond with good clarity, excellent color, and a significant carat weight will be one of the rarest and most expensive gems to be had.

CHAPTER 14

GOING INTERNATIONAL

THE ASSASSINATIONS OF DR. MARTIN LUTHER King Jr. and Robert F. Kennedy put the nation into a state of collective mourning. Nothing made sense anymore. And I was still missing Babe.

It was 1968. Rhonda was sixteen, the age when she really needed a mother. She didn't want to be living alone at her father's without a woman around, and after Babe died, I didn't want to be living alone at my house, so I picked up my daughter from her father's home in West Virginia. Ronny had just turned twenty. He would soon be sent to Vietnam. I now knew how my mother had felt, sitting at her kitchen table talking to herself when the military took Albert, Clarence, and David to fight a war for a country that could just as easily lynch them. I couldn't get Mom's words and frustrations about my brothers out of my mind—

because we knew so much more about the war now—and I carried mother's worry about what would happen to Ronald.

When I arrived in West Virginia to pick up Rhonda, I found myself wanting to just be home. I remembered the smells and the sounds of the birds, and the lack of stress felt comforting. I went to Keystone, West Virginia, the small predominantly Black town where Rhonda lived with her father, in the middle of the night, when the fog hangs in the valley the way it does. I hadn't seen Rhonda in a couple of years. I walked into her bedroom and called her name. She sat up in the bed, and all I could see was her grown-looking shadow, but her voice still sounded like my little girl. "Mama?"

When she climbed the stairs to her new room at my house, I followed behind her, hoping I had done good. She put her hands over her mouth. "Ooo, Mama!" and jumped onto the white pillows. It was the room of a princess.

Things went really well for the first couple of weeks. Then I enrolled her at Shaker Heights High School, and the stress of living in a city and trying to fit in really got to her. One night she came into my room and didn't ask me but told me, "I'm going out with some friends."

I sounded like Mom. "It's nighttime. You're not going anywhere."

She wasn't a sassy teenager, but she sure slammed my door and yelled, "I'm going back to live with Daddy!"

I drove her right to the bus station the next morning. A young woman has got to have some control over her own life and make up her own mind. If that's what she wanted, I was going to give her a hug, some money, and let her go. A few days later, she asked me to come get her again, and that was that. She settled into her Shaker Heights life, and my life felt grounded again with her there, and with Mom a stone's throw away.

I DIDN'T HAVE Babe as a connection anymore, and I was a known criminal, so I had to figure out how to be a single working mom whose career had new challenges. The good thing was I had plenty of money in the bank. *Doris, maybe you need to cut out the stealing shit and be normal.* I would go down to Mom's house and play cards or go to the speakeasy to hang out with Shirley or Kenneth. I felt empty.

Shirley told me, "You have Kenneth, and he's a fool about you. Make something out of that." Dudes talked about him bad in the speakeasy, how he was so into me that he could barely mind his own business. They called him "King," but I said, "I'm not gonna call you that unless you call me 'Queen.'" Most nights we smoked ourselves high and laughed and teased each other like two kids having a good time. About three months after Babe passed, things got sexual between Kenneth and me. I hung out with him weekdays when Rhonda was at school. It was unlike any closeness I had allowed with any man.

Crime was worse than ever in Cleveland, and after my

face hit the papers with the Pasadena incident, I had a mor-
bid fear of being robbed in my Shaker Heights home. I let
Kenneth know I needed his protection. "You want me to
come stay with you, baby?" he asked.

I did not pause for even a fraction of a second, snapping
back before he could even finish asking his question with
that smile: "NO! I want us to tighten it up."

Kenneth never raised his voice at me. He was the only
man I was comfortable telling about Vernon, my imaginary
husband, how I had practiced beating him to practice pro-
tecting my mom against my father.

MY MOTHER HAD found love again with a churchgoing
man named Robert Mitchell, who she had known for a
long time, but she hadn't let him across her threshold. They
eventually got married, and she went to church on the regular. She now had a steady life with a man who treated her
well.

One evening, Kenneth met up with my mom and Robert and me at a restaurant in the hood. I sat there watching
Robert, whom I called Stepdad. He and Mom flirted with
each other like teenagers. Out of nowhere, I busted out and
yelled at Kenneth, "If you ever put your hands on me, you'll
have to kill me! Just because I gaped my legs open doesn't
mean you own me!" Everybody looked at me like I had lost
my mind. Kenneth just smiled and said, "I'm not Vernon."

I went on trying to be domestic-like and hated it. Shit went on like that for three years. Everybody was happy, and I was happy for them. But my shit was all off. I needed to go back to work.

I told Kenneth about my heists. He just said, "I'll never understand it, but you go do what you have to do, baby."

And I did.

I had facial recognition in the United States. At first I thought that was a limitation. Once I got to planning how I was going to get back into things, common sense kicked in. *Shorten it up and go where diamonds make their first stop on the black market—Europe.*

From my studies during my West Virginia childhood, I knew some of the history of Monte Carlo. Monaco had royalty, and the country was home to some of the richest people in the world. I read about the royal wedding of movie icon Grace Kelly to Prince Rainier. Etched into my memory were the photos in magazines of the ornamental buildings that looked like royal palaces. I knew if I was going to begin stealing in Europe, Monte Carlo was the place to go.

To prepare myself, I stayed at the Hilton in New York, where Babe and I had stayed on numerous occasions. The staff remembered me and gave me the princess treatment. For three weeks I watched the women in Saks Fifth Avenue like a hawk, read the *New York Times* every day, and studied *Vogue* to mimic the fashions and memorize the most valuable jewels.

I entered Monte Carlo in late summer of 1974, the same

day Nixon resigned, and the same day the first Black model, Beverly Johnson, appeared on the cover of *Vogue*.

When I got off the airplane in Nice, France, I knew I didn't have to worry about the police at the airport because of the news focus that day. I was the only Black person in sight other than that *Vogue* cover, but my attention wasn't on that.

I took a cab to Monaco. It was so gorgeous to drive through the spaces of wide-open skies above valleys, rows of hills, and evergreen trees like back home in West Virginia. For the short thirty-minute ride I experienced mountains that descended to the sea. As we entered Monaco, there were yachts with their masts sticking up like pins out of one of Mom's pincushions. To my left, the high cliffs of chalky limestone looked no different from the limestone cliffs and mountain passes of West Virginia. I thought, *Chile, you have come a long way from taking the bus to Pittsburgh.* We drove through a small tunnel, and there it was: the wealth of terra-cotta-tile roofs piled on the hillside right down to the Mediterranean Sea.

I arrived at Hôtel de Paris. This was the real shit, a palace-looking building that was hotel and casino in one. There were palm trees in front, and the building had statues of naked goddesses. I was in my element again.

The young bellhop said, "This way, *madame*." There were buttoned-up upholstered sofas, pillars, fine oil paintings high above my head, and a stained-glass window of the heavens. I thought, *Hot damn!* But I still kept my nose in the air as I followed the bellhop into the elevator and to my room.

I opened the French doors to the port, smelled the salty air, lay on the chaise lounge, and laughed out loud. "Sweet Baby Jesus!" On the coffee table was a leaflet. *Cartier of Monte Carlo.* These people were begging me to get a piece. I fell asleep to the sound of Louis Armstrong jazz wafting up from the outdoor terrace below my balcony.

I woke to the squawking of seabirds. I could've lain there all day. But I had come to do a job and get out of there. Room service with eggs Benedict, a hot shower, and my best movie-star outfit. It was a slim-fitting cream-colored linen suit jacket and skirt that I had gotten from Saks. It hugged me at all the right places and stopped just below my knees. I put on my cream-colored pumps, grabbed my handbag and my big ole sunglasses, and was off.

While the concierge hailed me a cab, patrons entering the casino glanced at my teardrop diamond earrings, my tiny teardrop green emerald necklace, my wedding rock, and asked, "*Qui êtes-vous?*" The more of them who asked who the hell I was, the more of them craned their necks like chickens to see the movie star. One man stood out like an American sore thumb just like me. He was a square-faced, long-haired white fellow who looked like he could afford to defy the fashion code. He dressed like a hippie in a slouchy shirt and jeans. We held each other's gaze for a moment, and then I got into my cab.

The driver asked, "Destination, *madame?*"

I said without hesitation, "Place du Casino." It was in the fine shopping district. The narrow, steep streets had shops on both sides, reminiscent of San Francisco. Except the signs were in French and the streets were much narrower. I knew just enough French to get by. Mom had been raised Catholic. Without a place to worship in Slab Fork, she had recited the priest's part and the congregation's part of the Catholic Mass while doing the dishes. Those Latin roots had given me just enough. On the streets, I didn't see one Black person, but I was all right holding things down for my people in Monte Carlo.

When we arrived in the shopping district, I realized we had traveled away from the hotel and come back to the same area. I could have walked. But I couldn't get into that kind of cheap thinking. Going on foot the few blocks would not have been becoming for a woman of my stature.

I strode the few yards across the sidewalk. A store jutted out at the corner with wrought-iron and decorative elements. Cartier made the statement that it was the finest jewelry store in the world. Just before I reached the door, I noticed the same poorly dressed American hippie I had seen at the hotel walking up the street. We caught each other's eye for a second. I wondered, *Who are you?*

A female shopkeeper stepped out of the store to lock it for her tea break just as I was about to approach. Break time was the best time to switch things up and take what I needed.

"Oh my. You are closing?"

She turned to me, and I saw that her eyes didn't question. She registered that I must be famous.

She couldn't resist a potential sale and smiled. "Come right in, *madame*."

A young male server came to the door to welcome me off the sunny street and into the chandelier light. The place had Belle Époque décor. There were velvety black displays of diamond necklaces and glass cases with black velvet tubes of diamond bracelets. I saw what I had come for. Glass cases with big-ass rocks. The only problem: I was the only customer. This might make things complicated. *I'll look today and take tomorrow.*

The female shopkeeper made me comfortable. She motioned for the young male server to bring out a selection of rings. There was one glass coffee table, where we sat, and another taller table to my right. The server placed the tray between the woman and me, then went off for a second tray, which he held like he was a butler or something. He knew the rules and knew not to put it down until he could swap it for the other tray.

That's when the American hippie entered the shop. Something about that dude made me nervous. But that's when the server placed the other tray with five pieces on the taller table to go and greet him. Big mistake.

I engaged the lady. "Oh, my husband's sister has a piece like this. It is so beautiful."

She did not realize that the server had placed the tray there. I watched every move she made and every move he made, waiting for the gap when neither of their eyes were on me or on the tray, then I reached forward and put the largest rock on.

When the server returned, he was aware that there was a piece missing, a ten-and-a-half-carat, $550,000 round diamond ring—that's a $2.5 million diamond today. He looked at me and smiled warmly. I pointed at the shopkeeper to indicate that she was still working with me. She clearly had taken one of the rings to show to me. He was not about to ask for it while his superior was doing her job.

Now I had to go. I couldn't run out the door, but as long as he didn't say anything to her, I knew I was cool.

"Oh, my driver is here, and there is more shopping to be done. I'll come for a piece tomorrow." I knew I had a small window of time before they would recognize they had been robbed. I quickly walked right out the same door I had come in.

At that time Cartier was the premier jeweler in the world. They had been in operation as a family business in France since the 1800s. They are known for having made jeweled tiaras for King Edward VII and for receiving the appointment of half a dozen royal courts in Europe. For the first time in their history, a woman walked into the store, was shown a selection of jewels, and had the nerve to walk out the door to go about her shopping day. All the while wearing one of the most valuable pieces in the world.

I did not take a cab. I walked the short distance back to the hotel, packed, and headed by cab to the Nice airport.

My first mistake was to make my move in the store when there was only one other person shopping. The second mistake was that I didn't change my clothes before heading to the airport. I left a visual trail for anyone who came in contact with me. The airport was still abustle with the news of Nixon's resignation. I was able to catch my breath. I checked my ticket. I had a long wait. This is when I made my third mistake. I chose to wait. This was not a Greyhound bus station where I could get my shit together and leave when I felt ready. I had a half-million-dollar ring on my finger.

I learned the most important thing that day: an international jewel thief has to get into the air, off the ground, out of the jurisdiction of where she stole. Get anywhere as long as it's a flight out of the country where she took the damned thing.

I glanced up at the clock again. A woman and a man in Air France uniforms approached.

I knew they weren't real police, so I went with them willingly. I took the stolen ring off my finger while we walked. They took me into a room with a metal table and chairs. Like a good jazz musician, I was going to have to improvise. *Pay attention to what is happening every second and find a way out of this shit.* I had two goals: keep the ring and get my ass back home.

When the man was on the phone, I asked the woman very politely, "Are you going to strip-search me?"

She said, "Yes."

I knew she didn't have a legal right, but I took out a

Kleenex and blew my nose. "It's cold in here. I know the floor is colder. Can I start by giving you my pantyhose first?" I had the ring in my left hand, got my pantyhose off, and gave them to her. She shook them. As I put my pantyhose back on, I folded the ring into the Kleenex and pulled it up into the back of my pantyhose. Then I took off one article of clothing at a time to stay warm while she searched each piece of clothing.

They took me to a different holding place in the airport while we waited for the French police. I asked the woman, "Can I have my fingernail clippers out of my luggage so that I can keep myself looking nice?" She looked stern and took them out for me. Later I asked her for a needle and thread to fix the hem of my skirt. I continued to be polite. She softened her stern look. I took down my skirt, took the ring out of my pantyhose, and used the needle and thread to whipstitch the diamond ring into the hem, where it stayed for months.

In the night, they took me back to Cartier. They measured my arms. I guess to understand if my arms were long enough to reach that counter from where I had been sitting.

Then they put me in custody. Not in a jail but in a holding place that was more like a bed and breakfast nestled in the hills of Monte Carlo. Women were there from other countries. I was restricted to my room while a man and his wife sat out in the hallway and brought me what I needed. I got to look at a menu every day and order what I wanted to eat.

I loved the scenery. The balcony was right over the Mediterranean where Elizabeth Taylor and Richard Burton had once vacationed. I could look out on the yachts and hear jazz playing just like my first night in the city. *Okay, I can live like this. Let the waiting game begin.*

During those first weeks in holding, my thoughts drifted to my mom, who knew I wouldn't have left for more than a month. When once I had been in New York for three weeks, I had called her every night, but this was a long span of time without her hearing from me. I didn't worry about the kids. I knew Mom would cover for me, tell them I was out working. She would hold all of the worrying herself.

I wondered what Kenneth was thinking, but he was still new in my life. He didn't understand how long a European gig would take anyway. I found myself itching to read a newspaper. I needed some information from the outside other than what was on the menu or what the big band at the marina would be playing that night. I listened at the door to the man and woman and their visitors. Much of my additional understanding of French was developed by eavesdropping on my hosts.

One day I heard them gossip about me and the hippie American man, the other customer in Cartier, who it turned out was Jann Wenner, cofounder of *Rolling Stone* magazine. Apparently, he had gotten in touch with the US Embassy, trying to find me. It wasn't any of his business, but I think he desperately wanted to understand who I was and held on to the situation like any journalist would, like a dog with a bone.

Often a woman came from the US Embassy who had

been assigned to visit me since it was international law that the embassy make sure I was okay. She was a tall, blond, serious woman, but the more she got to know me, the more she smiled and relaxed into something near friendship. I begged her for updates about anything, any news from the outside. She showed me a copy of a deposition Jann Wenner had voluntarily offered to the French authorities. He said he came into Cartier because he saw me earlier that day and wanted to know who I was. He'd never seen a Black woman in Monte Carlo, let alone a Black woman enter a Cartier.

At first I was livid, but I realized that I had benefited from his presence. I would not have made the move had he not come in. He hadn't been detained. But as far as they were concerned, he could have stolen the ring just as well as I could have. After all, they still couldn't find it. It had to be somewhere, and by now, they likely thought it was on the black market. Later I heard through my eavesdropping that Jann Wenner had gotten expelled from Monte Carlo because he had magnified the crime.

It was a stalemate. They couldn't find the piece and couldn't hold me forever for a crime they couldn't prove. Nine months went by. One day a man outside the door said, "The Americano is in there." He asked the other man, "Did you find the ring?"

He said, "She has it in there." He was just speculating, speaking the hypothetical truth. But it scared me to death. I was done waiting and needed a plan.

I remembered that one time a judge sentenced me to six

months in jail in Cleveland. I had never served any real time and was not about to. I developed some horrible stomach issue from the stress, and they sent me to a hospital emergency room. Babe contacted a lawyer, who got a statement from the doctor to present to the judge. The statement said I couldn't be in jail because of my intestines. I was set free after serving two hours in jail and twenty-four hours in a hospital.

When any of the women got sick in my Monte Carlo holding house, they had to take them to a hospital run by nuns. I figured if I could get myself to the hospital, I could take it from there.

The next week when the woman from the US Embassy visited, I already had packed my suit jacket, skirt, and the toiletries they had given me in a little bag. I was dutifully wearing the drab brown skirt and white blouse they issued all the women. I lay on my bed gripping my stomach. I had left untouched my dinner from the night before and my breakfast on the table next to my bed. The pudgy husband who owned the hostel tried to remove the old food that morning. But I said, "*Non, non, j'ai faim,*" making him think I would eat it.

The woman from the embassy went out into the hall and argued with the husband and wife for a while. Then a car came to take me down the hill to the little hospital, which was in an old Romanesque cathedral. They allowed me to bring my little bag of clothes so I could change when needed. I also still had on all of my other jewelry: my watch and forty or fifty thousand dollars' worth of diamond jewelry, including my emerald-cut wedding band.

At the hospital, I sat on the edge of the bed waiting for the doctor. A nun-nurse came into the room smiling, sat beside me, and said, "The doctor will be here soon, dear."

I reached out for her comforting hand, displaying my wedding ring. She sat up. "What a beautiful band you have on." She put her hand over the white collar of her habit and confided, "We are married to Jesus. A ring like that would show such devotion to him."

I held my stomach again.

She said, "Oh dear, the bathroom is right there if you need to go."

I sat there with her a while longer, then said, "I might as well take my wedding ring off. Here, you hold it, because I'm going to have to take it off anyway when they x-ray me." I gave it to her. She sat there distracted and mesmerized. Her body was angled just so. If I was quiet enough, she would not hear me leave. I grabbed my little bag, went into the bathroom, got dressed in my suit, and left the frumpy brown skirt and white blouse behind. I wanted her to keep the ring. If or when they figured out that I was not coming back, she would have the ring and might not want to impede me from getting away for a while. It was part of the cost of doing business.

I walked out of the hospital into the light as bright and beautiful as the day I had arrived in Monte Carlo. A Nigerian man unlocked his sports car. I went into a lying act.

"I'm here with my fiancé. He got stopped for drugs. I need to get to Paris. Can you give me a ride?"

It was going to be a hell of a long journey, but he went into action. I bet he thought he'd hit the fine-woman-in-distress jackpot.

I can't tell you how happy I was that afternoon to ride through those limestone tunnels, up and down those windy mountain roads, and out in the open farmland of France. When I arrived in Paris, the Nigerian dude gave me some bills to tide me over and asked, "What can I do?"

I was still going with the movie-star theme. I told him I just needed a night's sleep and to contact my agent in the States. He booked me a room in a two-star hotel—not the Ritz, but I was grateful. He asked again, "What else can I do?"

I knew by this point he was hoping for more. So I told him, "I'm so tired that I'm feeling like I need to vomit," and that was enough to send him on his way.

I bought a dull frock of a dress in the hotel gift shop and made a call to Kenneth. I didn't want to call Mom. I couldn't contact her until I showed up at her door, letting her know that not only was I all right but I was back.

Kenneth did not answer. *This man has probably moved on with his life.* I took a chance and called his mother. She said, "Honey, Kenneth is in New York. He thought he might find you there."

When he got in touch with me, I didn't go into any hysterics about where I had been for almost a year. I could tell he wanted to press me by the number of pauses and deep breaths I could hear through the phone. I got straight down to telling him what needed to be done.

"Send me five grand. Don't worry about getting paid back. If I can get myself to the States, I have you covered a hundred times over."

He had an adult daughter, Linda, who was very sophisticated and had a passport. She knew how to handle herself. She flew to Paris and came straight to my hotel. She brought me some extra clothes. I knew my Kenneth. He packed those clothes and packed money in the pockets of every dress.

Now I needed a passport. My passport was still with the Monte Carlo police. After I brainstormed with Linda for a couple of days, that Nigerian dude came back to check on me. I told him I needed help getting out of France altogether. I gave him $500, the equivalent of $2,500 today, and he went into action again.

"No problem." He took me and Linda to a motel close to the train station in Lille, France, so we could be in the largest city nearest the Belgium border. He said, "When you check in they will ask you for your passport. Tell them you have it fastened in your purse for safekeeping but can read them the numbers." Of course I didn't have a passport, so I made up a series of numbers.

He came to pick up Linda and me the next morning. We rode across the border of Belgium to Brussels with him lying that he was our driver and that one of us had lost our passport. He told us in the car, "That will work."

The sentry said, "Yes, yes," went into the booth, and

gave the dude a map with directions to the US Embassy in Brussels, where I could get a six-week emergency passport. All I had to do was remember the last place I had used it, which happened to be the hotel in Lille, and they would use that number they didn't know was fake to create my new passport. On the application, I paused before filling in "NAME."

For a long time jewelers didn't even know what race I was because of my light skin. The only time I gave a jeweler a name was if he shook my hand and directly asked my name. I then made up a name, whatever came out of my mouth. Most of the time I leaned toward something Arabic because of the association jewelers made with Arabs having money. I would pronounce some complicated name that sounded like I was trying to hawk up something. But for my passport, it seemed a lie closer to the truth if I used an American name. I filled in the name Thelma Creighton Wright. I thought that shit sounded like some rich woman.

Linda and I were astounded at how versed this Nigerian dude was in everything international. He and I worked like a team to get me out of France and into Germany without my real passport. From there, Linda flew straight home, but I was up in the air, off to one country and another before landing in New York.

Kenneth said, "Damn, baby, some people ain't got enough sense to get out of town, and you got out of France without your passport."

CHAPTER 15

DIAMOND FEVER

T'S HUMAN NATURE. IF YOU HEAR ABOUT SOME-body striking it rich on his farm in West Africa because he dug up a rock as clear as glass, you head your ass to West Africa. If you hear about some dude in California who found a gold nugget in a river, you head your ass to California. The problem is, that's not how you think if you're Black. If you hear some guy is rich with diamonds, you wait until some brotha tells you he figured out how to turn the diamond dust from the rich man's pocket into grocery money, and you get out your dustpan. But I was always the kind of Black woman who headed to the farm or the river where they found the diamonds and gold.

When I was still in Paris waiting for Linda to arrive, I gave Kenneth instructions to get some information. "I need you to put on your most clean-cut suit. Make sure you go get a haircut. Go to Van Cleef & Arpels on Fifth Avenue. Tell the man that you bought a piece for your lady and discovered she was making it with somebody. Tell them you want to sell it and get as much of your money back as you can." We laughed over the phone. "Really sell the story, Kenneth. Like the whore left you and you need to get your money back."

Men could relate to those kinds of woes. Also, I knew a fine-jewelry house like that wasn't going to buy it off him, but they were doing dirt like everybody else, so they would know where he could take it.

He paused and said, "My woman did leave me."

I didn't address that shit. His woman was working.

When I met Kenneth in New York, he reprimanded me. "See, I had to get you a change of clothes from your house. You were so scared I was going to move in on you that I didn't have a key. I could have been arrested trying to get in there."

I just wanted him to shut up and kiss me. "You're just fussing because you're glad to see me."

We made up, but I still wasn't going to let him move in. I had made some mistakes in Monaco and gotten waylaid, but I had come home with the most expensive piece I had ever taken. I had great confidence in myself now without Babe on the scene.

Kenneth said the clerk at Van Cleef & Arpels had been sympathetic and told him to go to New York's diamond district. He gave Kenneth the number of a stall, a buyer who knew diamonds and emeralds. Second to Cartier, a reference from this jewelry store was the most respected reference for sure.

The next day, I walked into 10 West 47th Street. I had never seen so many men in fine suits in one place. They moved around like worker bees.

I made my way to the second floor, where the jewelry supplier I was looking for sat in a six-by-six-foot space. Other men sat in their stalls, each one bent over a table. They examined jewels like specimens with small devices that looked like one lens broken off a pair of binoculars. I gave him the ring. "I'm selling it. What can you give me for it?" He studied the piece beneath a light that looked fit for dental surgery, then hunched over to place it beneath his little monocular. Under magnification, jewelers can detect black specks, cracks, or cavities that are not visible to the naked eye. These inclusions lower the clarity grade and value of the diamond. Cartier purchases only the highest-grade diamonds. I could hear him swallow as his mouth watered over the reality of what he had in his hand. He bought it for a tidy sum. We shook hands and he didn't ask questions. I didn't want him talking to me. I didn't even want to talk to him if I didn't have to. However, before I left his stall that day, he said, "Emeralds are beautiful on women with your color skin." I glanced back at him and held on to that truth. I knew he would be my new buyer.

KENNETH AND I remained in New York, hanging out at the Hilton. It was a whole different deal being there with him than it was being there with Babe. Kenneth was set on becoming a big-time promoter and was friends with Don King. I went on and on about my diamond business, which he didn't understand, and he went on and on about trying to be a boxing promoter. When Don King landed Muhammad Ali as a client, Kenneth was through too. He spent much too much time trying to get in good with Ali and push King out of the way.

I tried to impart to him some of the things Babe had taught me. "Hon, King has monied white promoters and a business head. Study what he has and get what he has."

Kenneth wasn't one to tell me to mind my own business, but there we were, in a leased hotel room with Ali, King, and a bunch of boxing promoters. They were having a good time, laughing and clowning around, but Kenneth was somehow thinking this would help him get in good. I had to agree to stay out of it, but Kenneth's envy of King got so bad that he had his boys on the street keep King from ever showing up in Cleveland. He just kept saying, "That nigga owes me. If it wasn't for me, he wouldn't have landed Ali."

I SPENT MY time in New York resting up and shopping for my next campaign, reading the paper and watching the news. Angola erupted into civil war. The United States and the Soviet Union warred by putting their African dogs in a pen to fight to the death. The Soviet Union put its money on the People's Movement for the Liberation of Angola. The United States put its cash on the National Union for the Total Independence of Angola. When the white nations got tired of losing money, they took the Africans' diamonds and oil in trade for weapons and split the riches.

I couldn't handle the rage I felt. I hadn't felt any shit like that since I'd held a pot of boiling beans over my father's back. I wanted the diamonds off my body, out of my house. And at the same time I wanted to swallow them like contraband.

I didn't feel one bit of reluctance about the four-day campaign I was planning on the jewelers of London, Paris, and Rome. My targets would be the flagship European stores that served royalty: Garrard & Company, jeweler to the British crown; Van Cleef & Arpels, jeweler to the French elite and the Iranian crown; and Bulgari, jeweler to Jesus himself, from what I heard.

London would be first. Garrard had been described in some of the novels I read when I was sixteen years old. There would be somebody playing a violin or some shit in the Mayfair shop. The jewels would be in a beautiful parlor while the main character, someone white, strolled in and was served by a well-dressed clerk.

I flew first class over the Atlantic for a second time in less than a year, in September 1975. I felt like I was reversing the current. I flew first class because I could. The white woman sitting next to me went on and on about her daughter, whom she had just dropped off at a US university. I listened, and did not listen, as I watched her wedding ring float in the air on her hand. By the time she finished her monologue, I had counted the more than ten carats scattered across her fingers, arms, neck, and ears. Once she had exhausted herself from talking too much, I relaxed and read the two newspapers in the seat pocket, the *Times* of London and the *New York Times*. They both held the story of Margaret Thatcher's trip to the US.

As the new leader of the conservative party in Britain, she was boasting about the need for a no-welfare state and the need to steer away from socialism. There was something in her tone that forecasted her win of the prime minister seat four years later. The chick was campaigning. While she was in the US, making herself known as an international figure, I made my way to her town to do some campaigning of my own. I let out a chuckle before allowing myself to doze off.

The London skyline could have been mistaken for Manhattan if it wasn't for the peaks and points of the buildings. The terminal at Heathrow was a stream of people coming and going, much like the Manhattan rush that always got my blood flowing. It was an unusually sunny day in London. I heard the city whispering, *Come get your diamonds, Doris*. At the taxi stand, I ordered a limousine. I wore a beautiful navy-blue, Jackie Kennedy–style, scoop-neck dress with three-quarter sleeves and a silver trench coat. I couldn't let an outfit like that be defamed by sitting in the back of some smelly cab.

When I pulled up at Claridge's, two doormen in traditional top hats waited to escort me into the hotel. The place was so Buckingham Palace. "Madam" this and "madam" that. In London, I was a queen.

Today I watch young rappers on TV and see the way they turn into men behind gold chains. Something about wearing that much money on their bodies gives them attitude, confidence. I understand what happens to them. My fashion, my jewelry, and that five-star London hotel gave me confidence, made me feel the regal inside me.

I woke the next morning to the sound of a church bell. It was disorienting at first. I thought I was hearing the Sunday-morning church bell in Slab Fork. I washed off the jet lag in the marble shower, then dressed in my new mauve linen suit and convinced myself to get out of the room and feel the streets of London beneath my feet.

I made my way down Old Bond Street to an ornate building. I was almost an arm's length from touching the building looming over me, one I had dreamed of standing in front of as a child. The square plate on the building read GARRARD & CO., LTD., JEWELERS TO THE CROWN.

Inside, everything was so proper. Men wore black suits, narrow black ties. In the corner between two big pillars, a guy in a full tux with tails tickled the ivories on a baby grand. He played sultry jazz, which set the tone to buy or steal. If I wasn't there to do a job and get out, I would have lit a cigarette, sat down, and listened to the music.

A young server approached. "How can I assist you?" He had big doe-like eyes, and my work whistle blew.

"I'm interested in emeralds and diamonds only." He

smiled and put out his hand. I put my hand in his. He took me into a room that looked like a ballroom with dark wood cabinets. *This dude and this music—both are all right with me.*

He opened a cabinet. "Here you will find our emeralds." He opened the next cabinet. "Here you will find some of our finest diamonds." He opened the last set of cabinets. "And here you will find both emerald and diamond pieces." He also pulled open a set of drawers that showed off the jewels on black velvet. *Jesus.* Having done his job, he stepped away toward the door. While he had his back to me, I reached in and swiped a pair of pin-backed earrings with a round emerald in the middle surrounded by ten tiny diamonds. Then I closed my fist around an oval-cut emerald surrounded by twelve diamonds. I plucked them from that drawer the same way they had been plucked from the mines. I closed the drawer of the two pieces I had just swiped.

When he reached the door, the clerk turned around. I picked up another small emerald with four tiny diamonds on a platinum band. I motioned for him. He brought me an empty tray like he was bussing the tables at some fancy party. We continued to walk, and he added to my selection four other pieces that he said I would love.

Once we were seated, I spent an hour sending him to get another piece and another piece. He did a pretty good job of keeping count. It was getting close to closing time. The lighting changed in the place like they were a club getting ready for the late-night crowd. The pianist changed to slow, sexy jazz. So this was how they seduced the last customers into buying something, anything. I took advantage of the mood and asked him in a tone like we were out on an intimate date, "And where might you be from? I wonder if I've ever visited. . . ." I thought asking him about his personal life might make him think I was really interested in him.

"I grew up in Wiltshire."

The dude couldn't keep his mind on what he was doing. He finally lost count and brought me more than he had intended. The store was minutes from closing. He still had a big ole tray out and a sweet smile on his face. I didn't think I had ever stayed in a place that long, but I enjoyed watching him fall for me. I had what I needed already. All the lust he felt would make a good drug to help him handle the reprimand *What do you mean you can't find the jewels?*

Finally, I went back to the small emerald and diamond ring. *Hell, maybe I'll take that one too.* We discussed price. I asked questions to keep his mind from being idle while I made another move. "Do you mail purchases to the States?"

He blushed and said, "Why don't I put together a collection and bring them to your suite?" I almost burst out laughing. *Bring them to my suite?* He sure did get ahead of himself. I told him I'd think about it and left.

I let him watch me gracefully walk out. Once I was out of his sight, I knew I needed to get the hell out of London because he would guess I was staying at Claridge's.

I didn't bother checking out of the hotel. They already had cash for a two-night stay. That was common for people who came there from the States who had exchanged their dollars for pounds. I got my luggage and hopped into a taxi that night. I was on a flight to Paris two hours after I had taken the jewels, not enough time for them to even figure out what had happened. On the plane, I drank a cup of water to relax, then spat the water back into my cup when I realized this time I really had forgotten: I had the diamond and emerald pieces I had lifted, but I was wearing the little emerald and diamond ring too!

THAT NIGHT I stayed at the Ritz Paris. It took my breath away to see a wide stone courtyard surrounded by a fortress of buildings. I imagined this same spot during World War II, people running across the square and into the buildings while bombs lit the sky. It felt timeless.

I had to focus on my plan. When I woke up in the morning, I would make my way to the Avenue des Champs-Élysées shopping district.

The next morning, I just lay in bed, peeking out from under the covers at the Louis XIV décor. I talked to myself: "Who the hell do you think you are? Coco Chanel stayed up in this luxury. You are out of control."

I don't know if I was experiencing some kind of mental breakdown from jet lag or what, but I told myself to cut that shit out and get up. I hadn't brought my ass all that way to get halfway through my campaign and quit. I put my hair up in a ponytail to hide my sweated-out edges, and I tied a fashionable red scarf around my head. I put on my best Audrey Hepburn–looking short-sleeved, slit-pocket beige dress and some dainty jewels and headed down to the lobby.

I held my head up and worked on my confidence in the elevator. In the lobby, I heard music coming from the wide-open patio lounge. The place had indoor fruit trees and shit that was so gaudy it was elegant. I made my way to a table, thinking, *What the hell?* I had to see this band. *What do these people know about jazz with that kind of funk up in it?*

A drummer, a saxophonist, and a dude getting down not on a piano but on an accordion. That put me back in the right mind-set. I had never seen no shit like it. The waiter asked, "Staying for tea, *madame?*" I sure was. I couldn't help myself. Between the music and the tray of croissants and beignets and shit, I considered ditching my campaign for the day and getting down with the Parisians. I drank enough tea to knock down the jet lag and get my head straight. Then off I went to do what I had come there for.

I walked through the hotel lobby with all of its tall, elaborate pillars into the court and found a Van Cleef & Arpels right there in the square. *Damn, that's convenient for international jewel thieves.* Almost too convenient.

It's the dirty little secret of long-standing family-owned jewelry stores: diamonds that become a girl's best friend are smuggled by Indiana Jones types. These young white business opportunists venture into the ongoing domestic violence in Central African countries, purchase diamonds from the cartels that fund the weapons of war, and get the hell out with the smuggled goods the same day. They look like regular vacationing travelers and are not questioned. They then fly to Antwerp, Belgium, which is like the coastal slave capital for diamonds. There the gems are mingled with the rest of Africa's diamond exports and are cut, polished, and sold to the big jewelry houses in Europe. But I didn't need to go into the middle of a war zone. The diamonds sat right there outside my hotel, waiting for me.

At first, it was uneventful. I set about my usual routine with a young male clerk. Then his manager interrupted. He was a broad-headed, older Frenchman with wavy, graying hair. He smiled almost too hard. "Good day, *madame*. I would love to be the one to show you our finest."

He wanted me to see watches. *Why watches? A woman comes into your shop wearing expensive diamonds looking like Lena Horne and dressed like Audrey Hepburn, and you show her watches?*

He brought out way too many without me trying to confuse him. There were women's watches and men's watches. "Something perhaps for your husband?"

I didn't like the situation. I didn't know if this guy was setting me up, but I wasn't going to let him have the upper hand. I said, "Yes, my husband would love to see watches from this year's line."

He smiled and got up to get yet another tray with three already sitting in front of me. I knew from years of training that if I felt like the clerk was likely to confuse me, then I needed more in my court to help me confuse him. There was a woman with curly blond hair nearby in a cute jumpsuit. I said, "Look at this elegant line of watches."

"Oh yes," she said with an American accent.

Damn. I had hoped she was Swiss or something. She sat down beside me like we were old girlfriends. We tried on a few pieces. She slipped on a women's dainty watch and held her wrist up in the air. I picked up a men's white gold watch with eight tiny diamonds and two rubies in the watch face that were more blood-red than my head scarf. I slipped it into the slatted pocket of my dress. When the man came back, he said, "Oh, you have a friend." She and I giggled and continued to look at the watches together.

I said to her, "Well, I have to meet my husband. Let's connect in the restaurant tonight for dinner. I would love to meet your husband." The manager watched us interact as if something was slipping out of his hands.

She said, "I didn't get your name."

In my most proper accent, I said the first *D* name that wasn't Doris that popped into my head. "Diane." She let out a little squeal as I walked out of the shop. I almost belted out a laugh when I realized she thought I was Diahann Carroll.

I didn't stick around to do any sightseeing. About an hour and a half later, I was on a plane to Rome, with a $55,000 Van Cleef & Arpels watch in my luggage, equivalent to a quarter-of-a-million-dollar watch today.

Much later, when Interpol was tracing my international

dealings, they interviewed the manager at that jewelry store. His statement read, "Yes, the nigger was here."

WHEN I WOKE up after a long night in the plushness of silk sheets and pillows, I felt refreshed but confused as hell about where I was. It took a minute. I went to the window, opened the drapes, and saw in the distance the Piazza della Rotonda. I stretched, satisfied. "I'm in Rome." The Eternal City, my last stop.

When Ronald was four years old, Mom watched him one night while I took my very pregnant self to the theater to see Audrey Hepburn in *Roman Holiday*. The movie had been filmed in Rome amidst the ancient ruins and streets filled with cars and people on bicycles. I planned to mimic her fashion the minute I got my figure back. I returned to the theater and watched that film three times. I could speak perfect Audrey Hepburn Italian: "*Taxi, per favore. Il conto, per favore.*"

I put on a simple green dress, one as form-fitting and as eye-catching to rival Sophia Loren, slipped my rings on the outside of my gloves, grabbed my long cigarette, and went out with the confidence to do my job well. I sat in a restaurant that morning with a view of beautiful orange blossoms. The waiter came to me twice in his white jacket and bow tie and asked if I wanted to wait for my husband. "*Il vostro marito?*"

I shook my head both times. I shook off the thought of

Babe and me at a similar place in Florida a few years ago. Finally, the waiter took my order. He treated me as delicately and as respectfully as royalty.

I didn't plan to make a move that day. I needed more sleep to get over some of the jet lag. It had been only seventy-two hours since I had left New York. Being a super-bad chick is one thing, but this was a bit crazy. I decided to go out on foot and see what the area had to offer and continue my campaign the next day.

I walked the narrow stone sidewalks of Rome's tight streets. In the shopping district, it was easy to imagine the days of horses and carts. The buildings had shops below and tiny terraces above with shutters, wrought-iron railings, and oil lanterns that extended out from each tiny terrace. The street I was on sloped up to an old cathedral-like building at the end. It brought to my mind the Wall Street district in New York. There were tall, modern buildings, but at the end of the street, a big steeple reminded everybody that the colonizers were here.

I had to tell myself that as beautiful as the city was, I wasn't there for a history lesson. I knew from the maps I'd studied in the hotel that Bulgari was just ahead. I needed to set a plan for the next day, walk by the place, and get a feel for the flow of foot traffic in and out of the store.

I slowed my pace as I reached Bulgari. Each display window of the shop had beveled dark marble surrounding it. I paused too long. The doorman had spotted the attractive Black American woman, or maybe he had spotted my dainty necklace with ten diamonds set in a V pattern.

"Good afternoon, *signora*." He ignored the other people walking up and down the street. Now that he'd laid eyes on me, I couldn't back out and return the next day.

This was nothing like Cartier or Van Cleef & Arpels. Inside, the African green marble walls were accented by tables and doorways of white travertine marble with deep veins of the Congo running through them.

I was inside the fault line between Africa and Europe. I hadn't felt that walking into the stores in London and Paris. I didn't want to feel that, because it was a distraction, but I felt it anyway.

I talked to myself while maintaining a calm, elegant exterior. *Get it together, Doris.* The clerk led me to a private parlor with gold fabric pillow-cushioned chairs, one for me and one for the clerk. *Focus on the clerk. Does he have any attractive features?* His accent was charming, some Italian-Swiss mix. "Where is your husband today?"

Damned if I wasn't sick of being asked that. He tilted his head to one side while his eyes furtively noticed my wedding ring, which over the years I had upgraded to a diamond-encrusted band and a big rock.

I blushed back. "Out on business."

This young man was dark-haired with lips as big and luscious as a brother's. *Sexy.* Another male clerk, who looked similar, walked in and out, bringing whatever my clerk directed. There was a little table to the side, where they poured me a glass of wine and a glass of water. Of course I drank only the water. Like the sexy clerks, the wine did wonders for sales, I was sure.

This young man really challenged my skills. He caused me to have to turn up my instincts a level. He had stuff brought out in droves without me even confusing him into it. This store did not have the same policies as others. Their tactic for sales was: drag her into the back room, get her drunk, and lay jewels everywhere so she will purchase to her heart's content. He reached for my hand and said in that accent, "Did you like anything I showed you?" This dude was trained like a stripper, but I was gonna find a way to flip it on him.

I asked him to bring back the tray that had the ring with a yellow diamond in the middle and teardrop diamonds around it. I tried it on, along with other rings. I made sure not to put them all back where they belonged. I left some on the marble table. I wet my lips now as often as he wet his. I got him. He didn't notice my hand move like a snake to the tray and slip the ring onto my middle finger.

I giggled about consuming too much water, and he pointed me in the direction of the powder room. I knew he watched my ass walk away. "I'll be right back," I flirted. I looked at the door. The doorman opened and closed it. "Good afternoon," he said to customers. I heard rain on the stone sidewalk. Leaving in the rain would ruin my press and curl, but it would increase the amount of time for me to vanish on foot.

I walked slowly and confidently out the door. I blended into the crowd of tourists headed to the cathedral-looking building at the top of the hill. At the cathedral, I hopped into a cab, told the driver to wait while I went into my hotel room, and changed into a much more casual traveling dress and hat to cover my already tightening hair. *"All'aeroporto,"* I said to the driver, and I was gone.

The first flight leaving was to Syria. At first I thought that was an insane choice, but I felt paranoid. I was carrying what would amount today to nearly one million dollars' worth of Africa on me. I hadn't felt my confidence dip until that moment. I just wanted to go up, off the ground, out of the jurisdiction of Rome. So I bought a ticket to Syria because I was willing to go anywhere en route to home, as long as it wasn't Russia.

I landed in Syria and caught a flight to Iran, a pattern that wouldn't make sense to anyone trying to track or identify me. In Iran, as long as I kept my mouth shut, I didn't look much different from the people of that region. From there, I took a long eighteen-hour trip to New York, rested up after the flight, and headed to West 47th Street, where I stirred those gems back into the black market and took my cut. Then I got myself as quickly as possible to Cleveland.

CHAPTER 16

RETURNING TO BABY JESUS

AFTER FIVE DAYS, FOUR CITIES, THREE CONTInents, and more than thirty hours in flight time and transit, I finally arrived home. I let go of the weight of the world when I saw Mom sitting on her porch. Before I could say hello, she said, "The police aren't following you, are they?" She headed into the house for the rest of what she planned to say to me. "I want you to do some honest work for a living." She held her face like she was in pain, her lips pressed tight together, her eyes squinting like she was hoping to see something buried deep in me.

I did what I always did—looked right past those concerned eyes. "You want me to be a maid?" I believed a woman shouldn't have to bend over backward to get the respect she deserved. I didn't believe in putting myself in subservient positions. As long as I was willing to follow the truth of life rather than the rules of life, a good life was always within arm's reach.

She turned away from me and wiped the kitchen counter in circles. "I'm trying to have a conversation with you, Dink."

I did what I always did in defense of those concerned eyes. "I'm trying to say hello to you, and you're cutting into me about what I do for a living?"

She wiped the counter harder. "Something could happen to Rhonda or to me, and what am I supposed to do if I don't know where you are or when you comin' back?" She raised her voice, which for her wasn't very loud. "Do you know what it's like, Dink, when some strange white man calls on the phone and says he's from this or that investigative agency and asks do I know where my daughter is? Do you know what it's like to swear before God in heaven that I don't know where you are because I don't?" Her voice trembled, and she smacked the dish towel on the counter. She still wasn't looking at me.

Like a toddler, I wanted to put my arms around her. I didn't want to see my mom unsteady. I was afraid of being alive in a world where the woman who held my life in place quaked with tears. "Mom!?"

She talked above my pleading. "You know I would protect you, but there's something about not knowing where on God's green Earth you are."

I tried sweet-talking her. "I'm right here, Mom."

She turned around and said, "No, you ain't, Dink."

She held her hands up over her head with the towel still in one of them, like the women who praised God at her church. "Thou shalt not steal, Dink." She shook her head and let the tears flow.

I reached for her. She backed up.

When I was little, Louise told me if I saw a pretty butterfly and bit its head off, then wrote a letter to Baby Jesus asking for that same color of dress, it would be mine. I was so excited that I could do just a little thing like bite a butterfly's head off and Baby Jesus would give me the pretty things the women had in the magazines.

I wrote down my request: "Dear Baby Jesus, please let Daddy stop being mean to Mom. Please also send me pretty dresses and things I need for my play kitchen." I put it in the postbox with no stamp and sat in my playhouse with the doors open. Eventually I saw a blue-and-white polka-dot butterfly flitting across the purple clover in the grass. I waited for it to land on a flower near me. I pinched its wings, brought it up to my mouth, and bit the head off. It was about the most bitter, god-awful thing I ever tasted.

The letter was in the mail. The head had been bitten off. I waited for weeks, but Baby Jesus didn't give me a damned thing.

"Mom?!"

She wiped her face with the dish towel and walked past me without touching me.

We were broken.

❧

ON SUNDAY, I went to church with Mom and Robert. It was a sanctified holiness storefront church—so you know there was a bunch of banging on the piano and people catching the Holy Ghost and falling out. If I didn't get religion out of it, I sure got entertained.

I laughed out loud, clapping to the music. I didn't have to worry about anybody recognizing me as a criminal up in that place. Half of them were stomping up the floor, doing the holy dance, and the other half were waving handkerchiefs and speaking in tongues. Robert got the Holy Ghost and got down on his knees, rocking and swaying and popping up and down, praising the Lord. His muscles tightened, and his knees got so messed up he was on painkillers and out of work for the whole week afterward.

They liked having me around, and I didn't care nothing about God and Baby Jesus, but I liked being in the middle of what they had. It felt like when I was little and would squeeze myself between Albert and Louise when they were sitting on the porch. Sandwiched between them, I felt safe.

Mom and her friend Mrs. Dennis had a ritual of sitting on Mrs. Dennis's porch on Saturday and drinking Blue Nun. Mom loved Robert but wasn't about to give up her lady drinks for religion. She invited me to come along. I accepted the invitation and drank me some ice water while those two got funky drunk. I had Mom lean on me to get her back across the street. It felt good having her body weight next to mine. The love between us was thick.

The next morning, I called her bright and early. "Time for church. You and Robert ready?" I knew what I was doing.

She said, "Dink, I think I'm too sick to go."

"Oh no you don't. Thou shalt not steal? Well, thou shalt not drink either."

She laughed through her hangover. "You got me there." It didn't matter what we had been through. I was hers and she was mine. We could always laugh our way through shit.

I heard Robert in the background, coaxing her. "Come on, Clemmy. I promise we won't stay all day."

I had to see that.

Through the preaching, Robert and I kept looking at Mom, waiting for her to upchuck or something. She held out the best she could. She got to sweating, and the last song came to a close. Then the pianist started feelin' it. The people were singing and a-hollering. "Yes! Yes, Lord! Hallelujah! Hallelujah!" People got to running around the church like they were on fire. The pianist banged so hard on the piano I could smell the mold on the inside wafting up into the commotion. The sister who always brought her own tambourine got to beating it out on her meaty palm. Mom looked like she couldn't take it anymore and like she saw an opportunity.

She started moving her hips and held on to the church pew like she was gonna fall out. She waved her hanky in the air and looked up to the heavens. I knew where she was going. I yelled, "Sister Mitchell is *feeling* God!" I let her fake-faint herself down to the floor. She found her way out of that shit.

Robert had to play along. He struggled with his bad knees to pick her up. We got out to the car and he said, "You can quit now, Clemmy. Ain't nobody lookin'." Mom and I repeated her moves over and over as I drove them home. She and I quieted down, then busted out yelling, "Hallelujah!" and we got to cracking up again.

Robert was too much of a gentleman to do anything about it, but he sure was mad. As of yet, he was the only person in my life I hadn't bought anything for. Mom hadn't told him what I did for a living. Robert thought I had some job where I traveled overseas with my boss. I thought he knew, though, and just preferred not to ask and not to know any more. Mom had told me he was raised in a family that treated him like dirt because he was light and almost white, and the family was involved in all kinds of crime.

I knew he wanted to trade in his old gray Plymouth sedan and get a great big black Cadillac town car. Mom said she didn't think a man of his age ought to have a car like that. She got tight with their money and said she wasn't going to help him. *Why not let the dude have what he wants?*

That evening, I swung by his job at Babcock & Wilcox at quitting time. I took him over to the Jewish funeral home where I bought all my other cars brand-new but off the books. He showed me the car he wanted. I went in the back door and came out smiling with the keys. Robert hopped into his new car and drove back up to the house with me.

All week Mom wouldn't so much as smile at Robert, and certainly wouldn't ride in that car. I don't know if she thought she was punishing him or punishing me. On Sunday she had to go to church, so she made an exception. But, she told him, she wasn't gonna be riding like she was with a chauffeur. Robert was so proud of his big new ride that he agreed to swing by and pick up the mother of the church, who was a seriously large woman. She had to get through the passenger door in back, and Robert held it open for her. Mom said when she looked in the rearview, Robert was trying to fold her up and get her in there with all that weight on her backside. Finally, Mom broke her silence. "Robert, what's wrong with letting her in feetfirst?" Mom cracked up and finished with being mad.

I lay in my bed that night laughing to myself about those two. I tried to imagine myself doing that every week. Maybe it would have worked had there been something else to hold me in place. Kenneth sure as hell wasn't coming to church with me. He didn't understand that any more than he understood my campaigns. He came over on Saturday and grilled out on my patio with Mom and Robert, but at the end of the evening, I sent him home the way I always did.

CHAPTER 17

FAULT LINE

T WAS OCTOBER 1980. I WOULD SOON TURN FIFTY. I went over to Mom's for breakfast one day after Robert went to work so we could plan some way to celebrate my milestone year. We had just finished laughing our asses off again about Robert getting the mother of the church into his car. Mom sipped her coffee, and I figured she was about to tell me her birthday idea. I didn't want any big shindig even though that's what she might be cooking up in her head. Maybe she and Robert and me and Kenneth could go see B.B. King in concert. I loved that man, and she did too.

But that's not what she had on her mind. "Dink, I think maybe you can find some work here in Cleveland. If you really try." It's like she could feel that I was getting bored with church and mundane Cleveland life.

I didn't say anything for a minute.

"I'd rather make birthday plans, Mom. I'm living my life just the way I want to."

"Yeah, but are you and Kenneth ever going to get married?"

I didn't intend to jerk my head, but the bob that I wore shook in front of my eyes, and my coffee went down the wrong way. I looked across the table at her and got to choking, trying to clear my airway.

She came to my side of the table and pulled my arms up above my head to help get more oxygen into me. "Can you breathe, baby?" I wanted to stay like that for a minute, her holding me. I didn't want to get back into it with her crying over what I did for a living. I was a jewel thief. It was my profession. I would have preferred for her to lash out at me, or yell, or anything rather than question me in that way that pulled on my heart.

When I was eight years old, she told me to get her a switch. I had been overdue for two switchings and had just committed some other crime around the house. I launched into a debate. "Mom, do you remember the last time you gave me my licking? You gave me three too many. Can those count for the few licks I'm about to get right now?" I made that shit up to try to get out of it. It didn't work. Mom laughed and gave me my lickings anyway. Looking back, I was glad. It put an end to her being upset with me about whatever I had done.

I stopped coughing, and Mom eased my arms back down by my side. The smell of bacon fat and Chanel No. 5 from the folds of her body made me feel safe. She said, "I worry about you. You all over the place. That big ole house sitting up there and you're on planes going God knows where stealing. You a fifty-year-old woman. It's time to cut the shit out." She looked me in the eyes and squinted. Her eyes were gentler with age, but they were the same eyes that had peeked at me through the slats in the shed, wondering if the devil had planted a seed in her daughter. Then she said the thing that took root and made a mess in my head. "At your age, Dink, what do you get out of it?"

I huffed and shook my head slowly, trying to shake off the fact that she was judging me.

"Say something, Dink. Don't just sit there. I'm asking you a question about your life."

I tapped on the table like I was tapping a cigarette, except I didn't have one. I took my purse off the chair and rummaged through for a smoke.

"You gonna smoke in my kitchen?" Mom lit into me with more words that fed my doubt. "It's not *if* you get caught, it's *when* you get caught. Turn yourself in, Dink. Do your time. And while you still young, live a normal life."

Her words struck fear in me: *live a normal life.* They say nobody knows you like your mama. I hadn't told her that when I had worked at Euclid Manor the other girls would abuse those old Jewish women. One day one of the clients had asked for her purse. She loved putting on her makeup every day. It was the only thing she still had in her life that made her feel like a woman. Of course she looked like a clown with it on, but it was her thing. One of the stronger girls who was good at lifting the clients onto the commode decided she wasn't gonna give the woman her purse any-more, and smacked her every time she asked for it that day. I thought I would die seeing that. I told her to just give it to her, and her angry ass told me to mind my damned business.

Under no circumstances did I want a "normal" life—a normal, regular, everyday Black life. No way. Being humili-ated at work. Paycheck to paycheck. Church on Sundays. Regular clothes. Routine relationships that don't go nowhere. Absolutely not. Not Miss Doris Payne. I wanted more than that. I wanted nice things. I wanted to travel the world. Nor-mal was not me. Didn't Mom understand that I had a spe-cial gift?

I sat there with my nose up in the air and blew out long streams of smoke. I tried to calm my thoughts so I wouldn't blurt out some harsh rebellion. She didn't mind me buying her and Robert expensive Christmas presents—the coffee maker, a living-room set, the big color TV, and that big ole town car. She had forgotten that when we first moved to Cleveland I would slip her some money. She had never wanted the kids to see that. "Wait until dark and give it to me on the porch." She hadn't refused it, and it had gotten us to where we were.

She slid her chair up close to me, looked me in the eye, and called me out by name. "Doris Marie Payne, if what you do ain't stealing, what is it? God ain't gonna mince words when you trying to get into heaven. What you gonna do? Tell Saint Peter that you weren't stealin', *you were takin'*?"

What came out of my mouth was quiet but foul: "What you gonna do? Tell him you weren't drunk, *you were partaking of your lady drinks?*"

Mom looked at me like someone had taken something out of her heart. I felt the kind of shame only the woman who birthed you can make you feel. Out the back window, the poles for her tomato vines stuck up in the air, supporting the last few tomatoes on the browning vines. She got up and walked outside.

CHAPTER 18

OFF MY GAME

WOKE UP THE NEXT MORNING, AND FOR THE FIRST time I left the country without making a plan. I went to the airport with the intent to buy a ticket to anywhere in Europe. I did not tell my mother where I was going. The devilish little girl in me thought, *Let her worry.*

I didn't even look in magazines for a nice piece. I told myself to get a plan. But then I started thinking about Mom and just stared out the airplane window. On airplanes, suspended I don't know how many miles in the air, with plenty of room in first class, I felt the safest, like I didn't have to look over my shoulder for the police, because everybody suspected I was somebody and I was high above the scene of any of my crimes. I went to France. I was headed back to the Ritz Paris and got to overthinking it. *Are you trying to get caught? Why the hell would you go back to that hotel*

*where the guy is on the spy for the Black woman who took
the watch?*

I didn't leave the airport. I bought another ticket and flew
to Zurich. I just needed to be somewhere new. By then I had
been traveling for more than twenty hours.

In Zurich, the air was crisp, like the mountain air in
West Virginia. I stood outside the airport at the cab station.
As dusk shaded the sky with a swipe of pink and orange, I
took a deep breath, expecting that feeling I got where everything heavy was behind me and everything exciting was in
front of me. But I didn't feel anything at all.

I took a taxi to the Dolder Grand, an old castle hotel on
a hill overlooking the lake, famous for its celebrities, politicians, and businessmen guests. It was twenty minutes from
the airport and just as quick to the fine-jewelry shops—
perfect for my impromptu job. I checked in, dropped off
my bags, made a quick clothing change and refreshed, and
called for a car.

After some small talk, the Nigerian driver said in his thick
accent, "Lots of nightlife in Zurich, lots for you to shop and
enjoy."

*Shop? This is Switzerland. The perfect place to campaign
on fine watches. I plan to enjoy my first nighttime heist tonight.*

When I was little, Mom said, "Louise, Dink, be in the
house before dark." Even today, if you're looking for me
and it's after dark, you know I'm in my home, not out in
the streets.

But that didn't have any bearing that night.

The driver looked into the rearview mirror. I told him, "Take me to Bahnhofstrasse." That is the main drag in Zurich's shopping district. I saw his eyes squint into a smile, "Come now, a fine lady like you has to have some nightlife, not just shopping."

I thought about it a moment, what the hell. I didn't really want to be alone, and I needed something to lift my mood.

I was dressed in a Diane von Fürstenberg emerald-colored wrap top and skirt, with a Christian Dior black crocodile purse and my red head scarf, the colors of the Pan-African flag. Mom used to say, "If you feel sunken, dress sassy, and your feelings will catch up with you."

We went to a rooftop place just off the main drag and were seated at a table under a drapery of light bulbs. This smooth-faced dude was handsome, and tall and lean, with a pretty white smile.

"A drink for the lady?" he asked.

I had never had no alcohol in my life, but I told myself to quit worrying about me and Mom and enjoy his company.

"Sure." I made him laugh with his mouth wide open when I said, "One bourbon, one scotch, one beer."

He said in that thick accent, "How about a kir royale instead?" That sounded good, a lady drink like Mom would have had.

We laughed and drank, and I was surprised at how relaxed I felt after a few kirs, not like drunk, just light and free.

"You come with me tonight to Davos where I will deejay at a club."

Davos, Switzerland, was the nightlife party spot and was just over an hour-and-a-half drive from Zurich. On the one hand, I thought that's just what I needed, to let loose to get out of the mind-set that had me feeling off my game, but on the flip side, I didn't want to leave Zurich empty-handed.

"Listen, how about we go back to the shopping district, you wait for me, and then we'll go to Davos?"

I was feeling good after those lady drinks. I strolled down Bahnhofstrasse. A little speaker from one of the shops was playing Diana Ross's "Upside Down." I don't know if I was dancing, but in my head, my body was moving to the music. The lights on the streets made all the foreigners—the Europeans, the Arabs, and the Asians—look so happy. I stopped at windows and checked out the merchandise but didn't go in. I kept hearing Mom's voice: *It's time to cut the shit out. At your age, what do you get out of it?* I said back to her, *"Woo, don't bring me down. I am having a good time."*

I stopped at the Rolex window and admired the watch on a pale brunette mannequin's wrist. The mannequin flipped her hands and struck a new pose. I thought I had lost my mind for a minute, then I realized she was a model—a live mannequin. I laughed out loud at myself. I looked past the model at the bright shop lights, watches on cream-colored satin sparkling as bright as a row of diamond rings. It was like a magnet that drew me in.

I smiled at the woman standing at the door.

"Welcome to Rolex." She had a beautiful Swiss accent. Then the scariest thing happened. I lost time.

I CAME OUT of the Rolex and saw my Nigerian driver. He cracked a joke or two about what I don't remember. I was looking around out the windows like I had lost something in the streets. I told myself it was okay, that alcohol can probably do that sometimes.

He took me to my hotel and waited in his cab while I changed into a casual dress. That should have been the moment when I said, "Go on without me, old girl hasn't slept in a couple of days and is feeling those champagne drinks," but I don't know if I was trying to prove Mom wrong or what. I hopped in and we headed to Davos, Switzerland.

I vaguely remember talking on the long ride. He kept saying, "No charge. Just some nightlife."

It wasn't a disco place, or a big nightclub. He was spinning some "rock around the clock" shit. I must have been out of my mind with exhaustion. I checked my coat and my purse. I was in the club and was trying to blend in, and decided to have another drink.

I was on the dance floor getting down. I forgot about my fight with Mom—hell, I even forgot about the Nigerian and was dancing solo. Then I just got a notion to leave. I don't know if my high was turning from happy to depressed or what. I was just done. I went to get my coat and purse to go.

I wasn't thinking. When the coat guy asked me my name, I just said out loud, "Doris Payne."

I was standing there shuffling my feet to the music and waiting. I turned around and saw a line of policemen. They were there for me from Zurich.

I was so drunk, I switched to another channel in my head. I said, "Doris Payne? That's not my name—that's what my friend Lydia's real name is." I started calling out into the club and stepping into the crowd, yelling, "Lydia! Lydia!" like I had some friend in the club I was trying to catch up with. The police said, "Bring your ass over here, bitch."

They put me on a train with a female police officer to go to French Switzerland where they have an embassy. This Frenchwoman was so little, looking like she weighed nothing but eleven pounds. She was supposed to police me? I wasn't even shackled, and was so drunk, I couldn't stop singing, "*One o'clock, two o'clock, three o'clock rock . . .*"

I don't know what was wrong with the police in Switzerland back then. There I was with my purse, in my traveling dress and smart jacket, looking cute like a passenger on that night train. That wouldn't have been the case in the States—my ass would have been shackled to the pole.

She got to talking. "You're my first client." She was all excited about nabbing the famous Doris Payne. She let me know that the reason we were on the night train was because it didn't make any stops. It must have been three or four in the morning. I started working that shit with my old

Monte Carlo getaway plan. I got to looking all forlorn and holding my stomach. She told me I could go to the bathroom. I guess she figured it was safe for me to go to the next car since I couldn't jump off a speeding train. Too bad for her—the train stopped for water and I got off.

There wasn't any light except the few dim bulbs from the station, and I saw a great big cornfield behind it. I was scared to death, but went running off in there, and the train pulled out without anybody getting off to come after me.

I came out the cornfield, and there were two cabs there waiting for the morning train to come through. My pantyhose had runs in them. I looked like I had been mugged. I must have been out of my mind. I told the cabdriver the only thing that was on the top of my head: "Zurich." I don't remember sleeping in any of that mess. I remember getting out of the cab and walking to the train station again.

I don't know how it was possible, but I had my luggage and I do remember I pulled my luggage through the train station in Zurich. I had clearly been back to the hotel because I was in new travel clothes with new pantyhose and my little raincoat. I almost passed out right there. I had to just stand still and get ahold of myself. *What the fuck just happened to me?*

It was like I was in a dream that isn't pieced together right. I had never experienced any shit like that and needed to get away from it. I caught the first train out of there. I fell asleep on the train. I woke thinking I had traveled far. Out the window, I saw a sign: LUZERN. I was less than an hour from Zurich. *Stay put, Doris, and get it together. Your ass needs sleep.*

I steadied my gaze on an older couple whispering and reading the paper together across from me. *Were they reading about me? Did I steal something in Zurich?* I couldn't even remember. Everything was a haze and the light of day was like somebody was taking an ice pick to my brain. It scared the shit out of me.

I snapped open my purse. There it was—a men's Rolex, almost identical to the Van Cleef & Arpels watch I'd stolen in Paris. I didn't know what the hell was wrong with me. *Maybe I'm too old for this shit.* I told myself, *Doris, get off the train at the next stop, sleep, and make a plan in the morning.* I was scared to death.

WHEN I WOKE UP, I could feel my body between the stiff white sheets of my hotel bed. That felt good, like I was whole in my body, aware of my surroundings. *I am Doris Payne. I flew to Zurich two days ago. I caught the train and got off in Lausanne. I am at a hotel in Lausanne, Switzerland.*

Plenty of times I had planned a seventy-two-hour campaign and hadn't slept for most of it. But one of my rules was never smoke any weed before a job, and I didn't ever drink, so that wasn't even a rule, but it was now. My main concern was that I couldn't get myself to remember what had happened in that store. I didn't know who had seen me, didn't know if the police were really after me or if I had dreamed all that shit about the woman police officer and the corn-field. I didn't know shit. Doing anything would be like do-ing a puzzle with missing pieces.

The sun lit up the linen curtains. I liked the feeling of my bare feet on the old wooden floor. I went over and let the light in.

I went into the tiny bathroom. The fixtures had slight rust. This wasn't the Ritz, and for whatever reason, I was okay with that. I looked in the mirror and almost didn't rec-ognize myself. I had dark circles under my eyes. *What the hell?* I reviewed my steps, counted backward to get myself to remember the Rolex shop. The little sleep I had on the plane was only four hours. The night before, I hadn't gone to sleep at all. Then there was a blank. Then I was in the Ro-lex store standing at the door. There was the Nigerian guy's face, some old-ass Jack Haley song in my head, the memory of the smell of damp grass, and I remember looking up at the stars. *Damn!*

Why didn't I just take a fucking *nap when I got off the flight?* My heart was pounding in my chest. I was mad as hell at myself.

Hissing and clattering sounds pulsed with my headache and drew me back to the window. I looked down. Between the buildings, a train swooshed by with the dinging of a bell, which repeated every thirty minutes or so, just like the sounds from the train trestle over our neighborhood in Slab Fork. I remembered hiding under it when I was twelve. One day Mom hadn't felt like waiting for the beautician to come to the neighborhood, so she went to Beckley to get her hair done, and the last bus didn't come back until ten p.m. I knew Daddy was going to be mean about it. So I went up to the train trestle and hid under it like a little troll and waited for her. I was scared someone would harm me, but I was more scared of her coming into the house late, alone, with Daddy mad at her. I felt safe there. An empty boxcar sat on the tracks above me and acted as my roof.

The nine p.m. bus came, and I watched, but she wasn't on it. I decided I was just going to pray she was on the very last bus. I refused to go back to the house without her, but I was getting tired. I climbed up a ladder into the boxcar, where I knew I would be safe, and fell asleep. When I woke up, it was daylight. I went into the house. I had missed it. Daddy had beaten her again, and Mom didn't even know that I hadn't been in the house overnight.

I let myself inch out into my day in Lausanne one sensation at a time. By midmorning, I had made my way to the very modest café of the hotel. The outdoor seating had little tables next to an iron railing that protected people from tipping over onto the railroad tracks below. I felt good nestled there in the cool autumn air. I ate a bowl of oats, nuts, and fruit in yogurt, and asked myself a shitload of questions. *Do you have your passport? Yes. Do you feel comfortable going to the airport? No.*

I spent the rest of the day walking the town. The sandstone buildings with copper and terra-cotta-tile roofs were beautiful in contrast to the deep blue of Lake Geneva, the fall colors, and the snowcapped Alps looming above. I wasn't into nostalgic shit, but it reminded me so much of the way coal-mining towns were built at the foot of a mountain, pushed right up against a body of water. I found myself wanting *home* and feeling fall in West Virginia when I thought of that word.

I laughed at myself. *You have finally lost it. Just walking around Switzerland like this is a damned vacation.* I strolled through the old town of quaint little shops and passed a few jewelry stores. I saw a whole scene play out, of blaring Swiss police sirens and me in handcuffs. I kept on walking. I spent a few days like that, paranoid but trying to push past that feeling. *Just take something and move on.* Without having the lost-memory puzzle piece of Zurich, without knowing what of my memories was a dream and what was real, I was stuck.

It got worse every day because I knew better than to stay in one city that long. In any profession, if a pro begins to doubt, they fall off their game.

I contacted Kenneth's daughter, Linda, in Cleveland, and asked her to help. She had made her way to Paris when I was stuck after Monte Carlo, so I knew she could handle herself. She asked, "You want me to call Dad?"

I asked her to hold my confidence and to just come. I felt like who I needed right then was a sister who knew my shit and didn't judge me. I told her to bring me some clothes that didn't look like my regular type of clothes. I felt like I could leave if I was in a disguise. She told me to meet her in Geneva. I was glad to take the short train ride to get out of my head and meet up with somebody who was going to help me out of this shit.

She brought me a nice-fitting pair of Jordache jeans, a pair of penny loafers, and a woman's pink Izod polo with a little sweater to tie around my neck. Everybody knew that I never wore pants. I told her, "I look like some washed-up tennis pro."

It was a great comfort to have her there. She stayed with me in Geneva for a few days until I could figure out what to do. Sure enough, I shook that feeling of paranoia and came up with a plan. I needed to get to another country first. I had been in and out of France by way of the Geneva–Chamonix route through the Alps. It was all mountains and snow, and folks were rarely stopped when crossing the border into France there. I didn't know if the Swiss police had a warrant out for me, but I knew once I was in France, I could get myself to Paris, hop a plane ten minutes after getting there, and fly someplace obscure, then to the US. I still had the passport with the name Thelma Creighton Wright. It had gotten me out of Paris before, so I was confident it could work again.

By then it was November, not the best time to travel the route I had in mind. The next day, I rented a Mercedes and hired another Nigerian dude to drive. He told us he knew of a place to cross where we would be fine. We headed for the French border, and it was snowing like crazy. The snow in those mountains was way worse than the blizzards in West Virginia.

The oncoming lane of traffic and the mountain face were on one side of the car, and on the other side was a railing to hold the cars in place if they veered toward the cliff. The driver sat with the steering wheel damned near in his chest. Whenever the car swerved a little, Linda, who was a stout, bossy woman, slapped him on the back of the head with her gloves.

Every time, he'd say, "I knooooow, ooookay, ooookay!" It got to be hilarious, which eased the tension, but it was a real-serious situation. I imagined a whole scene of Mom at my funeral, crying, "*I told you to cut that shit out.*"

When we reached the sentry station at the Swiss-French border, the guy checking passports didn't want to come out of the booth. He just shined a light through the snow. We all held up our passports, which of course he couldn't see, but he waved us into the French side. Again, the cunning intelligence of Africans in Europe got me through.

CHAPTER 19

THROWING DUST AT DISASTER

HEN I GOT BACK FROM NEW YORK AFTER being stuck in Switzerland, I went straight to my mom's house. I now fully understood what Daddy had needed when his leg got crushed by the slate that day long ago. He had wanted to be with his mother. I came back from Switzerland with my spirit crushed, and I wanted to be with my mom. She was always there when she knew I needed a mother.

I took Mom to see B.B. King in Philly. She loved being treated like a queen as much as any woman. Frank Lonardo let me borrow one of his drivers for the day. We rode up Broad Street in Robert's big-ass shiny black Cadillac like we owned the shit. Mom kept saying, "This is like going to the opera." She really got into the chandeliers and heavy drapery everywhere. Our seats were VIP in the first row.

People kept looking, trying to see who we were. One woman was like, "I'm telling you, that's Maya Angelou and Nikki Giovanni." Mom and I about died laughing, pretending like we didn't know which one of us was supposed to be which.

Man, when B.B. King got to playing, they knew who we were—two women who might as well have been in church. *"The thrill is gone. The thrill is gone away from me."*

I felt that in my bones and got to swaying. He sang out what I had felt when I was lost from myself in Switzerland. It was like some lover had left me stranded and disoriented. Mom stood up, waving her hanky, "Play, B.B., play!" We were a mess, just like everybody else in the audience. People whistled and clapped up in that opera house while B.B. tore it up on his guitar.

On the way home, we howled like B.B. *"The thrill is gone . . ."* The driver kept adjusting the mirror and smiling at us. Mom turned quiet just before we got to her and Robert's place.

"You tired, Mom?"

"My back is hurting me." She grimaced and made a groan, and I whispered, "The thrill is gone away," to make her smile.

A few weeks later, Mom made that grimacing noise again while we talked on the phone. Then she made a noise like someone was choking her. "Dink, my back is giving out." I told her to get the heating pad and lie down. But when I came over to bring her and Robert a take-out chicken dinner, she was sweeping. That was Mom. She made jokes just like me all the time, but that made it hard to know how bad things were.

After dinner, it was time to clean up. I said, "I'll do the dishes, and you sweep the floor."

Robert came back into the kitchen. He stood in the doorway rubbing his belly and yawning.

Mom looked me dead in my face and said, "Lord, Dink, I have a bad case of angina. I cain't sweep." We were still at the sink. She turned to the window with a smirk on her face. "Have you ever seen me with a broom? I'm telling you, you gonna have to do dishes and sweep."

"Lord, Doris, naw your mom can't sweep," Robert said. "I do all the sweeping and the dishes too."

When he said that, she winked at me and kept her lips pressed together to keep from laughing.

I whispered, "You ought to be ashamed of yourself."

"He said I couldn't sweep. I said I couldn't sweep. I can't sweep." She sounded like me.

FAKE ANGINA. Real angina. I didn't know, but I called that night to remind Robert to give her the heating pad and to let her have her hot toddy.

Robert called me before he left for work the next day. "She couldn't sleep, Doris. She was in pain all night." That morning, I drove her to the doctor. That was one long day with x-rays and a blood test. The next afternoon, Mom called and told me they wanted her to come back. I figured they had missed a test and needed to draw blood one more time.

We sat in the doctor's office, laughing about her veins running away from needles. Then a square-faced white doctor who looked too young to be anybody's doctor came in. "Mrs. Mitchell, you have very late-stage cancer in both lungs."

We didn't say anything. It was like we were trying to stay in the moment where we were giggling about veins. Both of us just kept staring at him. He sat down. "Unfortunately, this is common for people who lived in coal-mining towns. It's a form of black lung."

"Fuck!" I hadn't intended to say it out loud.

He kept talking. Mom didn't speak. I took the paperwork but I couldn't hear him. I blurted out again, "Fuck!" I saw Daddy kicking her in her ribs. That's what the doctor's words meant for me.

MY MOTHER HAD remained legally married to my father for ten years after she left him. Even though it meant he might come and fetch her or beat her. She had waited to collect as his wife on the black lung class action that all the miners from the Raleigh Company eventually received. That money had been distributed and helped my father buy himself a nice trailer and move back to Mount Airy with his family. Mom's tiny share had been spent more than twenty years ago fawning over her grandchildren and pitching in to buy her new house.

After the first round of radiation, Mom didn't show any signs of improvement. Her doctor said her body was too old for surgery and she would not be able to recover from it anyway. I didn't pay him any attention. I knew my mom. You couldn't beat her down that easy. They said she had a year. But two years into it, she was still laughing, using the heating pad, and sipping her Blue Nun. And I was still throwing money at the cancer.

I needed somebody to talk to about it all. Rhonda had gotten a job and moved to Columbus. Ronny was living in North Carolina. I went back to praying before I went to bed every night. But I felt like my prayers traveled down the hall from my bedroom into each of the empty rooms of my big house and turned into a whisper by the time God was listening.

Shirley was good to me during that time. She came around to my house and told me about all the crazy shit she was doing. When I got to listening to her, I didn't feel so bad being in my fifties and a mess.

My favorite story came one morning when she rang my doorbell looking half dressed with her hair tied up. I said, "Girl, come on in here before my neighbors see you coming into my house looking like the maid."

"Doris, I had a slip in judgment." We started laughing before she could even say anything more. She reminded me

204 / DORIS PAYNE

about a young fellow who used to come by her house selling stolen tapes. He was only nineteen, younger than Rhonda. I got to hollering, "Ooooo, chile," because I knew where this was going. Shirley and I used to catcall behind this young fella's back, "He is a fiiiiine lookin' nigga, ain't he?" and then laugh our asses off watching him walk back to his car.

Shirley said she had decided to help him out with his "business." That turned into a mess because she started sliding into bed with him. She was holding his hot merchandise for people she didn't even know, helping him find ways to move the shit, and "getting it" with him on the side.

Shirley was a hot thing, but you couldn't disturb her money without making her lose her mind.

I knew this wasn't gonna be any open-and-shut conversation, so I made us toast and coffee, and she talked me through it. "Doris, my young blood and I had some words. I told him I wasn't gonna spend one more morning seeing him to the door and asking him for my money. I told him to empty his damn pockets and give me cash. He tried to act like I didn't notice that new Caddy he was driving. He had the nerve to say to me one more time, 'Baby, I ain't got it.'" Shirley was loud and mad now, pacing around my kitchen from the patio door to the table. "Doris, I told him to just stand there for me for a minute, and I calmly walked to my damned bedroom and reached in the nightstand for my gun."

Oh Lord Jesus. She done killed this dude.

"Doris, by the time he got to the driver's side of his car

to get on out of there, I had fired off three shots in the air."
She demonstrated him running and ducking, her shooting.
"Doris, I told that nigga, 'Don't come back!'"

We got to laughing so hard she couldn't finish telling her
tale.

"You done lost your mind. Messing with that young shit
will get you killed or get you locked up."

We sat down at the table, looking at each other with
our hair wrapped up. We were a long way from the woman
in the sportswear department and the woman looking for
somebody to sell her stolen jewels. We tried sipping our coffee but spat it back out, laughing at ourselves in a mirror of
each other.

"What the hell is wrong with us, Doris?"

"I don't know, Shirley, but you doin' some Bonnie-and-
Clyde shit. And I'm over here trying to figure out how to
stay away from stealing shit long enough to take care of my
mom." We laughed until we cried.

PART IV

CARAT

A carat is a unit of measuring weight and size; hence, "carat" actually refers to carat weight. A metric carat weighs 200 milligrams, and carats can be determined by points—100 points being to the hundredth decimal place. A diamond of 50 points is a .50, or half carat, diamond. The price of a diamond increases with the carat weight, because larger diamonds are rarer and more expensive. The visible difference in the size of a diamond that is .90 versus a diamond that is 1.03 may not be that great, but the price will be noticeable, because the one diamond is exceeding a whole carat. Diamonds of two carats or more are higher-valued pieces. However, pricing a diamond of any carat weight will be affected by the quality of the diamond's other three Cs—its color, clarity, and cut.

CHAPTER 20

SNARED

I ARRIVED AT MOM'S HOUSE RIGHT AFTER ROBERT went to work. She was sitting in the living room, not in the kitchen. I teased her, "Oh, we can sit in here now? You've been keeping it like the royal palace." She looked up at me, worried, and I thought the doctor must have told her more news.

"Sit down, Dink." I sat on the cream-colored sofa, and the plastic covering crunched beneath me. "I sat in here yesterday with a man from the FBI. He asked me if I knew where you were. He said you were going by the alias Thelma Creighton Wright. He was a nice older white fella not much younger than me." She trailed off, talking about what he was wearing.

"Mom, why didn't you call me yesterday? These dudes don't play around."

"He didn't know where you lived or else he would have gone there first."

I had used Mom's address on my passport. Now that felt stupid, if not cruel.

"What did you tell him?"

"I told him you were out of the country. He said that corroborated what the Cleveland police had to say." She put her hands on her knees like she was starting to feel pain. "He didn't seem convinced that me or the police were telling the truth, but he didn't pursue it."

She went back to talking about how he seemed like a nice fellow, how he could tell she was sick and asked her if he could get her some water.

I didn't like that. "Mom, you didn't let that man walk through your house, did you?"

"Dink, I ain't crazy. I told him my husband was on his way home and that I could get my own water just fine."

Shit was happening faster than I could figure.

"He coming back, Dink. You can't stay in Cleveland."

I CALLED KENNETH and told him the FBI was looking for me. He came by and sat with me on the patio. We smoked and figured for half the day. Then shit just kept falling apart.

I got up to answer the phone, and it was Shirley. She sounded distressed. "Doris, I'm moving to Chicago."

Kenneth heard me yelling at her on the phone and came into the kitchen.

I put my hand to the receiver. "Shirley talking about movin'."

Kenneth had already heard on the street that Shirley was in trouble. "Yeah, I didn't want to bother you. But down at the club, I heard some guys are looking for her because she's holding their merchandise and shot at one of their boys. I put some dudes on it already."

I told Kenneth I didn't need him worrying about me. I needed to have all the information on what was happening with my family. Shirley was my sister. We had each other's backs. That day had way too many pauses in it for me. I didn't need Mom or Kenneth pausing to figure out what I needed. I needed the damned info so I could put out the damned fires and keep the house from burning down around me. I called my daughter, Rhonda, who was like a niece to Shirley, and she drove from Columbus to meet up with me and Kenneth at Shirley's house.

Cars were pulled up in front of the house and brothas were coming and going. I thought she was in there dead or something. We walked in, and shit was all over the place, but Shirley walked around the house with a notepad and a pencil behind her ear like a damned auctioneer or something. I asked her, "Girl, what the hell you doing?"

She said, "Doris, I'm selling this shit and getting out of here. Those niggas ain't coming after me with guns drawn. By the time they come around, I'll been done liquidated it all."

Kenneth chuckled. "Shirley, you know you're crazy." He looked at one of the dudes. "Don't you think these fools are just gonna go tell Jackson and his buddies what you doing?"

Shirley took a wad of cash from some dude and handed him a big box of hot car radios, still in their packages. "It won't matter. I'm leaving in a few minutes."

Shirley knew not to mention Chicago in front of them dudes. She knew how to handle her shit, but I needed her here in Cleveland. When the house was emptied of men and most of her stuff and the hot merchandise, I said, "Can we talk about another plan?"

She said, "Sure, but you got to follow me to my closet so I can put my shit in a bag."

I made it up as I went. "The FBI has been over to Mom's and is looking for me. I don't want to leave, but maybe I can come to Chicago with you."

Rhonda, who was a head taller than Shirley and me, shoved stuff in Shirley's duffel bag and said, "Then I'm comin' too."

"No, Rhonda, you can't leave. They would know you're where I am, and you're much easier to track than me. I don't want you mixed up in my shit. I need you to keep going to work every day and to drive here every few days to check on Mom."

She wasn't having that. "I'm grown. I know what you do and how you do it. I know how to keep my mouth shut. Fuck going to work."

I told her to hush her mouth up, talking like that. I had skipped a lot of time in her life, but she respected me and admired what I did, maybe too much.

We came back out into the living room, where Kenneth

had swept up and put a pile of knickknacks in the corner. He didn't mince words. "I heard you, baby. I think it's a good idea."

I told him I wasn't asking for his permission. He nodded in that way that said, *Don't forget, you don't need to boss me around.*

I SOON MOVED into Shirley's condo in Chicago, and she made a promise that she would cut the street shit out. She landed a lower-level job at *Ebony* magazine. It wasn't quite enough to cover the bills, and I didn't have the benefit of getting a job anywhere. I told her I was gonna quit my shit too. But the truth was, I didn't know what the hell I was gonna do. Mom had bills that needed to be paid, and I planned on catching a bus to see her once a week. Catching a plane wasn't an option with the Feds looking for me. I was gonna need money to do all of that.

I learned a lot from Shirley. She had only her own skills to survive and God. That was the basic foundation she stood on. She was a scuffler. She didn't whine but took care of herself. Any time she felt like life was about to get the best of her, she came up swinging.

Thinking about my dilemma, I asked myself, *What would Shirley do?* When she got home from work one day, I outright asked her, "What would you do?"

She said, "I have an idea. Let's go get our hair done."

Our cab let us out in front of a raggedy place. "Shirley, where you got me going? This place is in the middle of vacant lots, liquor stores, and storefront churches. This is the hood."

She laughed. "I ain't no government bum. Just follow me. You about to get your hair done by the best beautician Chicago has to offer."

We sat up there under the dryers waiting for our shit to dry so we could get our press and curl. Lola, Shirley's beautician friend, who wore an Afro, came to stick her hand under Shirley's dryer to check on her hair. "That's your sister, ain't it?"

Like me, Shirley always let people believe whatever they wanted to believe. "Sure is." She gently pulled the girl's arm and pulled her between our two chairs. "Tell us about that dude who's got a little side hustle for you that you cain't handle. I got a place to sell shit and somebody to do the labor."

I thought, *What the hell, Shirley?* But I wasn't gonna mess up Shirley's reputation by jumping in the middle of her shit. It's important to know how to be a good sidekick when necessary, so I waited until we were back at her place.

We sat down in her kitchen over a couple of Swanson pot pies—neither one of us could cook. I told her, "You got to tell me what you got in mind. I don't fence shit, and I don't let nobody in on my diamond business."

She said that one day she was sitting in the beautician's chair and Lola told her about scraping powdered cocaine from the sides of bags for money. She said Lola had been working that gig for some weeks. But she was sick of the labor. She had about fifty bags with cocaine in them that had to be scraped with razors. She was supposed to get about $10,000. "Doris, Lola tries to be street, but she scared as a church mouse. Every time the police go by, she act like they there for those damned bags." I listened, thinking about Kenneth telling me that he didn't need to know about my jewel thief business but didn't ever want me getting involved with drugs like he was.

One evening he and I had come out of a club on the shady side of Cleveland and were walking past an old warehouse used as a drug house. This woman leaned out the door, trying to talk to me about buying some shit. I had never heard Kenneth raise his voice, but he stood between us and yelled at her like he was shooing away a crazy dog. "What are you doing? Get the hell away from her!"

I told Shirley, "I'm in. Just don't tell Kenneth, and don't give my name to the fella Lola is dealing with. I just want to get my cut of it. Without ties." I didn't like the idea of mixing my criminal activities. I didn't know how the drug shit worked, and I'd already learned my lesson with the passport situation. I could be as slick as silk in the diamond business and catch a case messing around in something that was not my calling.

Shirley showed me how cocaine adhered to plastic and taught me how to scrape those bags with a razor blade and get as much off as possible. I didn't want to get into it with her, but I told her, "You have done this shit before. Don't be actin' like it's brand-new when you got all this knowledge."

"Doris, I do for myself. You wanted in. I'm just trying to make sure you take care of your mom."

After a few months, Shirley got in deeper. She bypassed the dude she had been dealing with and started selling the scraped product directly to schoolteachers. She figured they weren't going to turn on her because they had careers and families to protect. I didn't need or want to know any of that shit—the less information the better. I just took my cut and paid my mother's bills. I pretended not to know the rest.

ON THE WEEKENDS, I visited Mom. I always bought her something nice, and it seemed like she looked ten years older every time I came. And every time, she told me how nice that FBI man was. I never heard Robert cuss, but one day he was helping her eat and said, "Clemmy, don't nobody want to hear nothin' else about your damned FBI boyfriend."

Three years into her cancer, Mom was still able to laugh and sit herself up. Though it took ten minutes for her to get there, she could get herself to the bathroom three or four times a day. One Sunday I watched college football while Robert was at church. My mom and I had a deal: if I watched her soaps, she would watch my sports. I wanted her to have something that helped her mind deal with the pain, like her rooting for a team and calculating who was gonna win what.

During a commercial break, Mom said, "You know, Doris, I don't think that FBI man really want you. Anybody with common sense would know not to just come on weekdays. He sit up here like he my white cousin or somethin' and say, 'So good to see you, Mrs. Mitchell. . . . Anything I can get you, Mrs. Mitchell?' I think he caught up in it. He know you ain't no harm." She tried to laugh and got to coughing. After a few inhales, she said, "I'm telling you, this is how that man takes his lunch break."

"It's okay, Mom. I just want to turn myself in, but I don't want to be away from you for a year."

"I know you ain't waitin' for me to die then gonna turn yourself in." She coughed a little and got it under control. "Don't turn yourself in, Dink. I ain't goin' nowhere. Shoot! Doctor said I wouldn't last a year and I'm sitting up here talkin' junk." I forced a chuckle.

The FBI didn't have me on any of the millions of dollars' worth of jewelry I'd stolen. For thirty years, every small arrest they'd tried had fallen flat. I had been in and out of jail like it was all in a day's work because they couldn't prove it was me, and they couldn't find the jewels. Babe had taught me a long time ago that with the right lawyer and the right connections, I could take my profession to the top. And I had. I would have found every gem and given it back if it meant my mom would get better. I knew that the longest amount of time I could serve for passport fraud was one year in federal prison, which would likely be reduced to a couple of months if I was polite and manageable.

"I ain't leaving you, Miss Clemmy." That made Mom laugh. I hugged her and tried to memorize the way that felt.

SHIRLEY AND I made a lot of money. But no matter how dressed up I got, there wasn't anybody opening doors for me, calling me madam, and kissing my hand for selling drugs. Mom's doctors just kept saying, "Miss Payne, all you can do is make your mother comfortable." I told Robert to let me take care of all of Mom's medical bills, and I did. I kept scraping the bags, thinking if I made enough money, somebody was going to change God's mind about the whole thing about Mom dying. I could go back to work internationally and life would make some damn sense, but sitting by Mom's bedside, I never felt lower in my whole life.

If you knocked Mom down, she just got back up. She was sick in her body, but her mind was just fine. By now she had been fighting against cancer for more than seven years. Robert had to pick her up and put her on the toilet, feed her, bathe her, dress her. The two of them were shrinking, and it was hard to watch.

One day she said, "Dink, I cain't leave you."

"Just hush, Mom. Let's just watch TV."

She said it again like she was trying to declare something for God. "I can't leave you. I don't know what's gonna happen to you. You don't know how to be without yo' mom. I know that."

I sat there wiping my nose like I had allergies or something, but I was fighting to keep the tears back. "Mom, I'll be all right. You can go. I'll be all right."

Robert stood in the door, looking like a beat-down soldier. He didn't say anything, just held the doorframe.

Mom struggled to get the remote to turn the channel and just said it again. "Nah. I cain't leave you."

THE NEXT WEEKEND, Robert told me, "You go to the party. You know Clemmy cain't be there, and I cain't be there, just go."

Rhonda was turning thirty-three years old. We called that the age of Christ, because that was how old he was when he died on the cross. If you could make it past thirty-three, you were gonna be all right. I didn't want to be there without Mom, but I didn't want to miss that moment in Rhonda's life, like I had missed so many others as a working single mother.

My daughter went all in and had her party at the Masons' banquet hall. We had chicken, coleslaw, rolls, a bar, and a DJ that had us doing the electric slide and whatever else crazy he could get all her drunk friends to do. It was the kind of party Mom had always tried to get me to have for my birthday, but I was never one for big shindigs like this. I didn't know Rhonda knew how to get down like that.

She was trying to shake her booty and keep her eye on her watch at the same time. "Mama, you got to get your bus. You got to go." In the car on the way to the bus station, we laughed so hard about her getting turned around on the electric slide, I thought I would pee my pants twice.

We messed around too long, and I missed the bus to Chicago. Rhonda and I stood around for a little while, looking at the digital bus schedule, trying to figure out if it was best for me to spend the night with her and get the bus in the morning, or wait three hours for the next one. Girls know how to take care of their moms. She pouted out her lips at me. "I don't want you to have to wait here in the bus station."

"That's sweet, Rhonda, but I can handle myself. Go back to your party." The intercom announced that a bus to Cleveland was loading at platform 11. That was all I needed to hear. I decided to go see Mom.

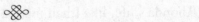

ROBERT OPENED the door. "Doris, I'm so glad it's you. I just put your mom on the toilet. I didn't want it to be any of the church folks." He asked me if I could watch Mom while he went to the drugstore.

Mom called out from the toilet, "Is that you, Dink?"

"I'll be there as soon as I get my coat off." I knew I could get her off the toilet if I tried hard enough. I was always able to figure shit out if I had to.

Robert said, "Lord, let me get her off the toilet first. I know you cain't lift her." Robert went to take her back to her bed. I was unzipping my boots, and I heard this god-awful, drawn-out, loud-as-hell moan. I rushed in, and he was sobbing, and he hollered, "She died, Doris!"

I didn't cry at first. I went and sat on her bed and told Robert, "Put her in my lap."

He placed her in my lap and ran across the street to get Mrs. Dennis.

I HAD SHIRLEY send me a big portion of my cash.

Robert and I saw a good white linen country dress with long sleeves and a high collar in the window of Rahall department store. He said, "That's Clemmy. That's her." I asked them for the dress in her size. They said they only had the sun-damaged one in the window. I told the manager, whom I knew, "It's for my mother who passed away." He had it dry-cleaned and sent it to the funeral home.

I picked out a casket, and the only flowers on it were mine because I insisted on only yellow roses. I used to give her yellow honeysuckle from out the yard when I was little. She would tease me and say, "This is sweet, but honey ain't money."

By the time my four brothers and Louise arrived, I had

taken care of Mom's arrangements on my own. They said, "Well, Girly always thought Mom was all hers."

In the church, the organist started playing, and that young lady opened her mouth to sing while everybody stood and made their way up to Mom's white casket to say good-bye. *"Why should I feel discouraged, and why should the shadows fall?"*

I saw Mom peeking at me through the slats of the shed. Saw myself holding the pot of beans over Daddy's back and her fallen body beneath him, felt the warmth still in her body when I held her in my lap.

I waited till last to see Mom resting in her casket.

Rhonda's voice was behind me, and I felt her hand on my waist. "Come on, Mama." But I couldn't leave her side. I felt the church empty and quiet around me, felt the sun change the shades of red in the stained glass. Then the ushers walked past me and closed the casket.

CHAPTER 21

TELLING PEOPLE WHAT THEY WANT TO HEAR

O N A MONDAY NOT LONG AFTER MOM'S FU-neral, in my house in Shaker Heights, I got dressed to head to the precinct and surrender Thelma Creighton Wright and her passport. Robert had called recently and told me that Mom's FBI boyfriend had come to the house again. Robert had told the guy the news of losing Mom and watched the grown white man break down like he had lost his own wife. The two of them sat and had coffee. "I'm tellin' you, Doris, this man sat there in his suit and talked about how much he understood Clemmy's devotion to you. I asked him if he was gonna start comin' every other day and questioning me next." Robert said the fellow shook his hand, went back to the front door, and told him that his job on the case had been to question the mother about the daughter's whereabouts, and that he had done his job. Robert ended with "Doris, I don't think he gonna pursue it."

"I'm a federal fugitive for passport fraud. They'll just assign somebody else. The nonsense will continue until they have me. I promised Mom I would do my time and get on with my life. I made her that promise."

I went across the street from my house and talked to Mrs. Gold before leaving. She was a nice old lady. When Rhonda was a teen, she and I used to go check on Mrs. Gold if there was a storm or anything. We sometimes brought her over to our house so she wouldn't be alone. I asked her if her son, who was an attorney, might be able to help me. I didn't tell her about my jewel business. I told her, "I lost my passport in Monte Carlo one summer. I didn't wait for my new passport to arrive before leaving. I have to do time in prison for a passport infraction."

"Doris, Jerry can help your family with whatever you need."

I surrendered at the Cleveland police department. I was in the Cleveland jail for only a few days. The police chief came to see me during that time. "I'm sorry for your loss, Miss Payne. I'll make sure you get the best treatment."

They put me on a sky-blue bus with fencing between the inmates and the driver, and then between the inmates and the door at the back of the bus. It was a long ride from Cleveland to the federal prison in New York. We stopped in some other cities and picked up other inmates, and that made the journey even longer. I never knew how many ways there were to lock handcuffs and shackles to things. Every time they moved the small line of women from one place to another, they chained us to posts outside in the parking lot, to the seats of the bus, to the water pipes outside the prison, to the handicapped rails in the bathrooms. I had never been shackled like that. I felt like I was Doris Payne the body without a spirit.

I went before a judge in New York for sentencing. He read aloud a letter from Attorney Jerry Gold, who spoke about me as an upstanding citizen in the Shaker Heights neighborhood. Though I had never met him, he wrote about the number of times I had gone over to his mother's house and assisted her as an elder in the community. The letter was written on Attorney Gold's personal letterhead, which I believe impressed the judge. He shortened my yearlong sentence to forty-five days. The federal attorney objected, but the judge's order stood.

I had never been to actual prison for more than a day or two and didn't know what it would be like. *Forty-five days? Doris, you can do this.* At least I would be made to be still and grieve so that I didn't fly away to be with Mom.

For weeks I felt lower than horseshit. I moved only if nudged or shoved to the next destination, to the mess hall, to the rec room, to my bunk. I slept on a bunk beneath a woman I never looked at and who smelled like sardines. Segregation was alive there. I was aware enough through my grief to notice that. We were all brown wearing orange. People told me this place was the princess prison. It was for the country's quiet offenders, who had committed educated crimes, like check fraud, tax evasion, and embezzlement. It was for us folks who couldn't survive in the same place with murderers and drug dealers.

I didn't count days, but after a while I started to feel again. The cafeteria smelled like eggs and dirty dishrags. The shower water never got hot, and the coils in my mattress left circular imprints on my back. Then I started to want things, like decent food, to have my hair done, to talk to somebody worth talking to. This was the only time in my life I regretted not getting married. If Kenneth and I had been married, he would have been able to visit me, but ex-convicts weren't allowed to visit federal prisons.

One afternoon, one of the male guards came to the rec room. I had never looked at his face before that day. I had just looked at his belly over his belt. "Doris Payne, you have a visitor."

Rhonda and a white man sat at a little round table with attached seats smaller than either of their butts. I was so glad to see my girl. It woke me the rest of the way up. She looked like a young version of Mom in her brown suit and makeup and glasses. I hugged her for as long as I could before the guard said, "All right!"

The white man was my attorney, Jerry Gold. I was glad to see him. "It's good to put a name with a face, young man." We shook hands.

"Miss Payne, you should be getting out this week. The federal prosecutor wanted to up your time. But you self-surrendered and have been no trouble. You served the time the judge set for you."

"Home"—I didn't like the sound of that word without Mom in the picture.

Rhonda read my mind. "They can release you to stay with me."

I've never put my shit on anybody. "No, I'm okay. I can go to my house."

When they left, I didn't like that I was now conscious of time. I wanted out. I wanted to be with my daughter and with Kenneth. I hadn't even felt the last month, but the next two days felt like torture.

The fucking Feds. They had me for passport fraud but had been in my house without a search warrant. Kenneth and I spent three days cleaning and cussing and counting what was there to see if anything was missing. I knew they weren't gonna be done with it just because Mom's crush was done with it. They had taken all of my jewels, all of which were purchased goods. The stolen gems were on the black market, not in my damned house.

Kenneth said, "Baby, I have folks who can take care of that fucker. I'll find out from Robert more about the dude that visited your mom."

The two of us sat on the patio. He drank his beer. I had a Coke. We stayed quiet until we'd smoked a whole joint. "Nah," I finally said. I stubbed the tiny butt out on a brick and blew out the last drag, which burned the hell out of the inside of my nose in a way that feels good. "Mom liked that blockheaded motherfucker. Don't do nothin'. The place is tore up because his brothers found out he'd turned on them and let the nigga go."

Kenneth sat up like it was time to throw his bet in for a fight. "I still got shit I can do, baby."

I got up from off that patio, ready. "They think they got the upper hand all up in my house and shit. I can go wherever I want. I don't need a damned passport." It felt good to be mad. I turned to walk back into the house. "Fuck, I ain't dead. I'm brand-new."

CHAPTER 22

TOKYO DIAMONDS AND THE MOHAIR COAT

PUT MY CLOTHES AND FURNITURE IN STORAGE SO the Feds wouldn't loot any more of my shit, and I went back to Chicago. I told Shirley I would scrape bags, and I did for five years, just long enough to get my shit together, build my wardrobe, find some confidence, and get back in the diamond game.

"Go 'head, Miss Doris."

I told her, "I ain't no government bum."

I had done it before—picked myself up from nothing, practiced, and taken back what belonged to my brothers and sisters.

Shirley and I were dressed to the nines one afternoon at a Chicago fashion show. Everything stopped for me when a woman pranced out onto the runway in a Karl Lagerfeld coat. It was a pin-striped mohair that had no buttons, just one hook. She had on a necklace that looked like six carats' worth of diamonds. I saw myself wearing that sweet teardrop diamond necklace with that dainty chain made up of round diamonds set in white gold. *Ooo Jesus*, and that $5,000 coat around my shoulders. That was one piece of fine-ass clothing, a good kickoff to my preparations.

Two years into it, I had everything I needed. While Shirley was at work, I sat on her patio, with fall approaching in Chicago. An ad in the *Chicago Tribune* caught my eye. Fall colors, luxury shopping. I could see myself in that booming, crowded city on that island, a hundred feet tall, like Godzilla, walking between those new skyscrapers in my mohair coat wearing my cute pair of Yoko Ono sunglasses.

That was it. Tokyo. I had never been there, and Cartier and their European brothers had gotten well-to-do enough to reach their rich asses all the way to Asia. Why not follow their diamond-dust trail and go on over there and get some nice pieces?

I was making my plan faster than I could keep up with myself. I went down to a Nigerian woman who had an underground documents business on the shady side of Chicago. I had seen state and federal documents from all over the place. Her shit was on point, right down to the type of paper and the smell of the documents. I pulled my hair back and put on a mess of lipstick. In my new passport photo, I didn't look like Doris Payne. I looked just like who I said I was, Audrey Davis. I had known at least three of them in my lifetime, so it was gonna be a while before the Feds figured out this was my new alias. They weren't gonna expect me to try that shit again. I felt that fire in me, and it felt good. The night before I left, Kenneth, Rhonda, and Shirley helped me celebrate my sixtieth birthday. I wouldn't let Shirley put my age on the cake. We shut the club down at three in the morning.

My cab pulled up at Tokyo's Keio Plaza Hotel, the one where they filmed *The Return of Godzilla*. I laughed at myself for doin' that shit, of staying at Godzilla's hotel. When I stepped out of the cab, I was a little shocked by the smell of shit. I learned later that the hotel sat over a former water-purification plant. The lobby was a mix of traditional Japanese and modern European décors. Once I got settled in my room, I looked out over the city skyline against the navy-blue and pink sunset and felt it: *Doris Payne is back*.

At the bar that night, I had a long conversation with a Japanese business executive who laughed too much, drank too much, and wanted to get under my skirt. "Many of the buildings here were built after World War II by American architects from your Philadelphia."

I had to steer his drunk ass back toward the information I needed. "Where can an American woman find a fine-jewelry store?" On my way from the airport, I'd had the cabdriver go past where I thought the Cartier store was, but when we passed through the busy shopping district, I did not see it.

"Oh, Cartier. It's the finest."

"Really? Where can I find it?"

He got to talking and grinning all at once. "Tomorrow I'll show you."

In the morning, I packed up and left my bags and a change of clothes in my hotel room, ready for a speedy departure. The Japanese executive met me in the lobby. He looked sober. I had hoped for that. He had ordered a limousine. "May I show you the fine shopping?"

I smiled, my mohair coat slightly off my shoulders, and I stepped into the limo. I had added something new to my international jewel theft rules: never come in the same car you plan to leave in. He was a gift to my plan that I hadn't counted on.

I smiled at him with all that red lipstick when he dropped me off in the shopping district. I told him, "I'm going to do my shopping. You drive around the gardens or wherever your heart pleases for an hour and then be right here for me." I knew this would keep him out of my business while I went to work.

He sat back in his limo, pleased, and nodded. "I'll be here."

THE STREET WAS like Times Square, but the shop was hidden up a long flight of beautiful carved wooden stairs. A young Japanese man dressed in evening attire met me at the door. Cartier anywhere on the planet is the same: French chandeliers and crushed velvet in red and black to make the diamonds pop. I was the only one in the store aside from the female clerk. And I actually didn't mind. No one knew me there. In 1990, it wasn't uncommon for a monied Black woman to walk into a luxury boutique in Japan. They would have at least one other Black woman come in that day, and the clerk wouldn't know one of us from the other.

The salesclerk wore a royal-blue close-fitting dress that was striking against her pale skin and dark hair. *These jokers over here definitely know some fashion.* She bowed slightly. "This way, ma'am."

Her hand waved across every drawer she opened, like Vanna White. Then she bowed and stepped back while I took a look at what they had to offer.

"Yes, yes," I said, holding up a necklace.

She stepped away to retrieve a tray. I knew she would. I knew their routine. I knew my routine.

I smiled at myself in the mirror, remembering how easy this was. I was in the place fifteen minutes. I complimented her. "Very nice selection." I imitated her slight bow and left.

I stepped elegantly down those wooden carved steps, and a white fellow came up the steps from the street. I knew he was the manager from the suit he wore and the authority in his steps. He stopped dead in his tracks when he saw me, like he had seen a ghost. I got a little shudder of doubt in my belly that I did not show. I told myself, *Doris, you aren't in his store. You're outside it, leaving it.* Then I got the shudder of doubt again as I reached the bottom of the stairs, *Doris, you have three diamond rings he can't see in your mohair pockets. If you get caught, you cain't claim that you "forgot" you were wearing them.* I kept tipping on down those stairs and sighed in relief when I saw an empty cab, which was a much better sight than the Japanese executive.

I got back to the hotel, changed, and was at the airport by the time my Japanese friend came back in his limo, happy after his time in the garden. I was in a plane halfway home by the time the French expat manager of Cartier figured out that the ghost and her diamonds were on their way back to America.

No going home and resting up from jet lag. I just got rid of the three rings. A square-cut five-carat diamond in a white gold setting, an oval emerald with tiny round-cut diamonds amounting to three carats in a platinum setting, and a big-ass sparkly six-carat diamond solitaire prong-set on a white gold band. Though I know I made my buyer on 10 West 47th Street in Manhattan a happy man that day, our only words were "It's good to see you again, ma'am" and "Likewise." I walked out of there with $300,000. Today, that would be a bankroll of a little more than half a million dollars.

I kissed on Kenneth and told him I had been to Tokyo. He about passed out. "Baby, you went all the way to Tokyo to steal some shit with all this shit to steal in the US?" That sounded like a plea to get me to stick around. A week later I flew to Greece for almost a year.

CHAPTER 23

THE LONG GAME

THENS WAS MY FOCAL POINT. I SET UP housekeeping there the same way I did in LA. I lived in the Astor Hotel on the thirteenth floor. It was beautiful, with views of the Acropolis from the restaurant. I could sit there having my breakfast, looking out over terra-cotta roofs, and right there, at the top of the mountain, was the shit I used to see in my head when I read about Zeus and Athena. I took the Acropolis tour. These narrow size 7AA feet of mine climbed the steps of the goddess Athena's home. I got to feel the sun on my brown skin in a spot on the Earth more ancient than Baby Jesus. I was the same Doris who sat outside my playhouse waiting for a blue-and-white polka-dot butterfly. I was a nigger in heaven.

Greece was historically fascinating to me, and had some of the best spots for diamond snatching, but Greece at that time was not a country for Blacks. You didn't see many Africans there, or many Black Americans for that matter. Not very much entertainment was there, because they didn't have nightclubs, which kept the rogues out. Unless you wanted to go on the water for some music, your best bet for entertainment was eating, sightseeing, and shopping. So I let Athens be my crow's nest where I could snatch jewels from the cobble-stoned pedestrian streets of the Plaka shopping district. I didn't sell my shit in Greece. From Athens, I would take my handbag full of jewelry and sell the pieces in Amsterdam, an easy six-hour plane ride away, where they had a jewelry district similar to West 47th Street's. All was in easy reach for doing my work, but I looked elsewhere for my social time.

I was just a two-hour flight from Cairo, Egypt. Every couple of months, I went, not to steal, but to vacation from my work and hang out. The low respect for women that American men have seems like the queen's treatment in Cairo, so I knew to stick to the tourist areas. I stayed at Cairo's Mena House Oberoi, which is now the Marriott. This place, like everything in Cairo, had a long history. It's where the peace talks between Egypt and Israel were held, and where many US politicians have stayed. The place was spectacular, with trees just like in Palm Desert, California, and outside my window, unbelievably, the pyramids. The first time I saw that shit I didn't know I was crying, but tears streamed down my face. I was standing before a sight that is as old as the Bible.

In Cairo, hashish was plentiful. It's illegal but part of

the culture. Anybody you ask is going to point you to some smoke. Men can sit in cafés and light up a pipe, but women can't do that, so I would have a few Ethiopian brothers I met over to my hotel, and we would talk shit and smoke pipe. Everybody who smoked talked real soft there, they said, because they had those pipes in the coffeehouses, and it was tradition for men to stay all day talking low so as not to attract the police while getting high. It reminded me of the origins of speakeasies—party past curfew but keep the constable away by speaking easy.

I was where I needed to be and stayed there nine months.

WHEN I WAS in Greece, I didn't communicate with anybody but my kids. One day, after I had returned to the US, I stopped by Shirley's for coffee and gossip. Some voice like an old woman's spoke from behind her door, all frail. "Who is it?" I figured she had moved.

I tried peeking through the peephole. "I'm looking for Shirley."

The door creaked open, and it wasn't Shirley but some shriveled-up version of her. The place smelled bad too, like piss. "Shirley?"

She sat with me on her bed, and I held my breath, trying not to smell anything or feel anything. She told me she had been in the hospital, but just like Mom, they had sent her home. Shirley's cancer was of the liver.

She had no one. She didn't have kids but she had me,

and I was so used to her doing for herself, I hadn't bothered to check in while I was gone. In this world, when you feel bodily alone except God, your survival tools are all you own. She was like that, never acted as if she didn't know she was responsible for herself. Typical Shirley, she had been released from the hospital and didn't think twice about taking that slow walk to Saint Peter's gate by herself.

I stayed for two months, cooked, cleaned. Did the things for her that I hadn't had a chance to do for Mom. I didn't leave her side. Then one morning she was gone.

She was like my sister. I was in shock, couldn't even cry. I knew I was going to have a delayed reaction, but I didn't get to, because two weeks later, Kenneth told me he had stomach cancer. All I could say was "No, Lord, please no."

I prayed for God to forgive me for my sins because surely he must have been punishing me for my lifestyle. I reminded God that I had tried to be in his flock but that he had kicked me out. It was like that conversation of "Remember that time you gave me three lickings too many?," but God wasn't feelin' me like that. I reminded him that I was the little girl who wrote so many letters to him that I would come to the dinner table and my father would tease, "Looks like we have an angel in our midst. She can talk to God."

Twenty-five long years. Kenneth was mine and I was his, and he had never asked me to be any different than who I was. God took him anyway. Kenneth didn't allow himself to be tortured, holding on till the last breath or no shit like that. He wasn't that kind of man. He took what was coming at him straight with no chasers. He was gone in a month. My world emptied out.

I couldn't even get grief to come bubbling up like a normal person. Instead, I acted up with God for the next thirteen years after he took my Shirley and my Kenneth. I hit every damn jewelry store in every damn state and didn't feel one damned bit worn out.

I would do shit like just ride to a mall as if it was a candy store and pick up some shit. I didn't have a plan. It was just a way to take back my power. Mom used to say, "Just because you can, don't mean you should," but I could, and it made me feel better.

On Good Friday I went to a mall in Akron, Ohio. I told the cabdriver to wait for me, and I walked into the place wearing a blue spring jumpsuit and my usual jewels.

It was a little mom-and-pop jewelry store, not my usual Cartier-type heist. The clerk was a sun-scorched pudgy man who perked right up when I walked in.

I looked in the cases, bored, but smiled occasionally at him and had him take out an assortment of rings to show me. The most expensive thing they had was a $32,000 tiny diamond ring. I told him some old con from back in my Babe days. I said I had just received my husband's $40,000 life insurance pay after his death a year ago. He said, "I'm sorry for your loss." But he had that watery-mouth look.

I sat down with the guy, and he showed me some pieces that I tried on. We chatted, I did my usual sleight-of-hand game with the rings, and I had the $32,000 piece on my finger. I ended our conversation and said good night. When I got to the door, he said something that no other shopkeeper ever said to me, "Oh, don't forget to give me back the ring." I thought that was the ghost of Mr. Benjamin or some shit.

I came back into the shop acting surprised. "Oh my goodness, can you believe we were so wrapped up in our conversation that we almost forgot about the ring?" We both laughed and I handed him the piece and we went back to talking. I wasn't about to mess up my perfect score. The cab was running up a tab, the other shops were rolling the gates down over their stores, the overhead music in the mall had hushed, and the two of us were still talking and playing with rings. One of us was gonna have to forfeit, and it wasn't gonna be me. I just needed to find his weakness. Each time he took my hand, he held it a little longer than necessary.

He began telling me all of his woes with his wife, the troubles they were having in bed and everything. I got to thinking, *You got to be kidding me. You gonna try to get in my panties? Uh-huh. Keep talking while I keep putting rings on and off my fingers.*

I just listened and engaged him deeper and said, "Well, it's getting late. Good luck with your wife." I got in the cab and got out of there with the ring on. Another one for Doris.

IN SPRING 2007, I sat up in my house in Cleveland, flipping through *Harper's Bazaar*, not to admire the fashion but to find where on earth was the biggest rock I could take. I wanted B-I-G, like a fucking glacier-size thing. A big-ass square-cut diamond was advertised at a store in a mall in Denver, Colorado. I was on a plane before you could say "Boo."

I was seventy-seven years old, but I didn't feel like that in my spirit. I opened the window at my Denver hotel that morning, smoked a cigarette, and headed to the mall.

Jewelry stores had resisted having security cameras the way white folks resisted integration. They wanted to maintain control over how they reported any missing merchandise. If you were going to have a store in a mall, you went by the mall's rules, not by the rules of your old-world European family. I wish somebody had told me about the damned new rules before I got a big surprise.

I went up in that store and walked away with that very ring, a $55,000 piece. I got back on a plane and headed to Philadelphia, because my brother Clarence was in a hospital, dying with brain cancer. I had accepted that was the way it was. I took jewels and God kept taking people, whether I lay down in the storm and gave myself up to him or I stayed hot, taking what I wanted.

Mom had said it ain't if, it's when I get caught, but my size 7AA narrow-ass Black footprints had been on damn near every continent, stirring up the rocks and scattering them to the four corners. I'd say I was successful, but there is always somebody playing a long game and hoping for snitches to carry out the deed.

I was in a mall in Philly and some dude called security. For a change, I wasn't actually there to steal anything, but in Philadelphia, good luck telling that to white mall cops. If some white dude pointed at you and said, "Stop her," that's what they were gonna do.

I didn't run, because I don't run. Well, at my age that wasn't gonna work anyway.

I reminded them that they couldn't hold me in their dinky little office for no reason, and they agreed. It wasn't ten minutes before Philadelphia police showed up. I didn't recognize them, because these were the sons and daughters of the men I used to have in my back pocket.

They drove me down to the precinct. They were very respectful and polite, and I had learned a long time ago to be the same way. I asked them in the car why they had me in custody. They got friendly. I probably reminded them of their grandmother. They said, "He recognized you from a fugitive Interpol poster he saw in the airport in Switzerland, and we just have to confirm via the internet that it isn't you and we can let you go."

Fucking Interpol and the internet.

It was me. At least I knew I wasn't dreaming about the tiny Swiss female police officer and my escape into the cornfield some twenty years earlier. But I couldn't be detained because there wasn't anything in the United States that said I was wanted. I had been cleared with the FBI and had served my time. Interpol had a twenty-page file they had continued to build through a couple of generations of workers. I had been twenty-six when they first got intel on me, amounting to some fifty years of campaigns, but they were an information-gathering agency, not an arresting agency. Turns out it didn't matter. Once my international dossier as a career thief came out, with descriptions of me like "coffee-colored brown," folks were mesmerized by the estimated value of what I had stolen over the years, and that I had never done any "real" time. I was considered notorious.

The Denver police where I had most recently stolen didn't have shit for evidence but issued a fugitive warrant to have me extradited out of holding in Philly. I guess they didn't want to be left out of the action. At first I was going to be transported by van, but they were really getting into the granny thing. The judge in Denver ordered I be flown out.

When I got to Denver, I was assigned a criminal defense attorney. I stood for my sentencing. The judge gave me three to twelve years. I thought carefully about who I wanted to call. The little girl Arfa who had been my brother Johnny's playmate in our first Cleveland apartment was now a federal judge. I called her and told her the extent of things—that Denver was acting way outside their jurisdiction, that they had nothing on me, that I was being sent to prison. I didn't know if she would be able to do anything or what that might have been, but she listened to the situation.

I stayed in the women's prison in Colorado for nine days. They said they didn't have the right facilities for a nonviolent offender of my age. They flew me home to Cleveland and released me to the State of Ohio for them to figure out what to do with me. Babe's best man at his wedding was in charge of all the prisons in Ohio. They released me into the hands of the people who wore the shit I had stolen.

The Ohio prison system didn't want me blending with their inmate population, bragging about my crime and tempting other women to attempt what was now my legacy. They sent me to a three-story old brick halfway house in Madison, Ohio, an hour from Cleveland, on the pretense that I wouldn't steal anything else.

The people who ran the house had a contract with the Cleveland police. They just had to report that they had seen me every day, and I had to say that I hadn't gone out of bounds by going into Cleveland or getting on a bus and leaving town.

I sat on the back porch every night, smoked, and watched the sun set. *Lord, how can your love be so cold? I don't know who gonna give up first, but I ain't never been beat down.* I bided my time, and they set me free after ten months of following the rules. Nine days in Colorado, ten months in a halfway house. I was lucky.

IN 2011, I flew to California, back to my old crow's nest, which had been renovated from a motel near the airport to an extended-stay hotel with nice new appliances. Los Angeles had cleaned up its act since the 1960s, dealt with the gangs, managed the drugs, but had a mess of freestanding jewelry stores that operated independently. They were in charge of their own shit so they could do things according to the movie stars they catered to behind the scenes. From that spot, I could get to Palm Desert, just southeast of Palm Springs, or Long Beach, or even San Diego, for a day-trip campaign. For three years I let the folks at the extended-stay hotel think what they wanted to think, that a nice old granny had come there to retire. I looked out on those palm trees every morning and went out from my nest, got shiny shit, and came home. The stuff I took was easy to sell; I had to just remember never to go to the same pawnshop.

I had a nice retirement-type life. My favorite thing to do was sit out by the pool with other jokers, mostly old Jews, and we would laugh our asses off about crazy stuff we had done as children. They were all survivors of some serious shit—from Auschwitz to persecution right here in the US—tough-skinned old bastards.

At that point I knew nobody in the world would recognize Doris Marie Payne at eighty-one as the same Doris Marie Payne at thirty-five, but a prison number follows you like a damned tattoo for the rest of your life. Those Pasadena jackasses couldn't let go of a grudge and came back to haunt me.

I was on a day excursion in Palm Desert and got too confident. I went to a mall that was all outdoor courtyards and palm trees. I was high on the weather, had my hair done, and was wearing a nice top-and-shorts set and some Louis Vuitton sandals. Most people thought I was in my fifties, not eighty-one. The jeweler was enjoying my company; I was enjoying his—it was as good as it gets. I hadn't met a clerk in a long time whose company I genuinely appreciated. It wasn't some granny shit. He was into me and wasn't bad-looking himself, had that Babe look of wavy black hair and a strong, broad frame.

Every time he picked up a ring, he took his sweet time, sliding it down my finger. I blushed, and it was hotter in that store than it was out in the desert. I left thinking, *Hey, I can still turn a head when I pick up a piece.*

I was feeling good and didn't go get a hotel. I caught a bus to San Diego and stayed two days. Got two pieces. Shit, I was on a roll. I headed back to my place and knew I was gonna sleep well.

I don't dream. I can count on one hand the number of times I've had dreams. That night I dreamed there was this owl sitting on my dresser. She was black with gold feathers and gold eyes, and she wasn't looking all wide-eyed and curious like owls do; she was scowling at me with her eyes. Her head was dipped down and her eyes squinted and heated up the front of my head.

I woke up to the sound of pounding on my door. I had on a T-shirt, no bra, and a pair of track shorts. I walked to the fire escape and looked down, and there were three police cars with their lights on. I stood still. *What you fixin' to do, Doris, jump off the fire escape like some granny action figure?*

"Miss Payne, please open the door. We know you're in there."

I took my time, put on a yellow spring dress, smoothed it out. Put on my new Louis sandals, some lipstick.

"Miss Payne?!"

I answered the officer like he was an impatient lover. "I'm getting dressed. I'll be right there." I put the rings in a package and put them where I had told the maid to look for her tip if I happened to leave early, like in handcuffs. I smoked the one joint I had in the place.

I opened the door with my head held high. I walked with dignity in that way my mom taught me.

Once I was processed and in holding at the Palm Desert jail, they didn't use my name, just called me by my prison number.

A psychologist came to visit and asked me why I did it. I didn't tell him what he wanted, some sob story about being a poor Black woman. I told him I did it because the jewelers wanted me to take the diamonds. "They want to be absolved of their guilt for selling diamonds that Africans pulled from the mines as slaves for guerrilla groups. They want me to take them so they don't have to think about the fact that their chandelier-lit diamonds finance weapons for the massacres of whole tribes of Africans."

He frowned like I was ruining his research. "You're a nice woman. Why don't you just talk to me about what I'm asking you?"

The trial took weeks. I contacted my previous lawyer from Colorado for help. He was generous enough to contact a colleague, an attorney named Blair Berk, who told me it was going to be a while. I wasn't an easy one for the judge to figure out. I was going to need to be in a facility where I wouldn't go teaching other women how to have the kind of career I had had. The judge was going to have to look at my harmlessness, my record of intestinal problems, and my psych evaluation.

The facility wasn't bad. Palm Desert jail had good food, gave me time outside, and even let me smoke out there. It wasn't some *Prisoner: Cell Block H* TV drama.

God was up by another point, but I wasn't done.

CHAPTER 24

DRY SNITCHES

ONE DAY THIS YOUNG MAN CAME TO VISIT ME. He said he was a film student who had seen my story in a local paper. Matthew Pond and I sat out in the visiting area. It was a nice space with windows, and you could see the traffic on the highway and the palm trees in the median. He was a cute little white boy in his thirties, but I was tight-lipped because I didn't feel comfortable with somebody who didn't know shit from apple butter saying they were going to make a documentary about me.

On his first visit, he told me about his project idea and asked me to think about it. He was my only visitor other than Attorney Berk. I was way the hell out in California, where my people couldn't get to me easily. On his second visit, he pulled out his purse-looking briefcase. This white boy had done his homework. He had black-and-whites of my mug shots and a few thick sets of files.

I said, "Now, wait. This looks like some kind of investigation."

He said, "I'm sorry, Miss Payne. I don't mean to offend you. This is just my research."

I backed off again until the next visit. He was persistent. There was something confident in the way he presented himself—not the snake type, more like the Babe type. Strong in character, the kind of fella to have your back, because he had integrity, and that was currency.

I signed a release and agreed to help him make his movie, figuring he would help me tell my story. I wanted people to know why I did what I did. I even told him about Mr. Benjamin and about driving to Philly with Babe to prove to him that his brothers could have the wool pulled over their eyes. He questioned me over and over, saying, "That sounds a little unbelievable. I'm going to have to review my research more."

"It's God's honest truth. Check it out for yourself if you want to."

We met every day for a couple of weeks, and eventually he brought another young white fellow along to help him get my stories down. We all laughed a lot together.

What I couldn't see from inside the jail was that this young man went to interview the man in the jewelry store in Palm Desert. That fellow didn't want anything other than his insurance money. He wasn't pursuing me, the state was. But Matthew told him that he had seen the article in the paper and told the jeweler, "I think it was my girl," meaning me.

I was released from the Palm Desert jail to a halfway house for probation, and Matthew continued to meet me for filming. I can't totally fault him. I enjoyed the attention. It was like being the movie star people had always assumed I was. "Put on this outfit. Show us how you walked in a store."

I signed out of the halfway house to meet up with Matthew one day. I was bored with the same questions and had gotten over the movie-star attention. It wasn't my job, so I decided to go to the mall instead. The next morning, he confronted me like I was his child. This little white boy acted like I had some obligation to him. I think it chapped his ass that I wouldn't answer to him. I was who I was. I wasn't about to change because he wanted me to act reformed for his documentary.

Attorney Berk wasn't able to continue with my case and recommended another attorney, a real sharp young white woman who looked at everything. She felt like they didn't have anything but the video camera footage, which showed a brown woman from the back walking up to the counter. One would have to speculate that it was me, but you couldn't actually see this woman's face. Matthew kept sticking his neck out like Jann Wenner, offering his opinion like he was some expert on me just because he had spent time filming me, and I had spent time answering him with what I had wanted him to hear—and with what he wanted to hear and believe.

For two years I was in and out of court, waiting for the

actual hearing. When the day came, summer 2013, I asked God if he felt I should stand before him in judgment. If so, I felt he should stand everyone who had acted against me in judgment too. That morning I had a bowl of oatmeal and wore my cute beige short set to take my judgment.

The door to the courtroom opened, and there were folks far back in the gallery. There were white folks I half remembered from one store or another in California, my attorney, and the state prosecutor.

It was a long day of questioning. Most questions I answered with another question or a politician's answer:

"I'm not clear. What is it you are asking me?"
"I did what anybody would do."
"I used my common sense."
"I forgot I was wearing it."
"I don't know where these other jewels are that you're speaking of."
"That isn't me in that video."

One of the jewelry store clerks resorted to tears and pleas to have me put away no matter how old I was. Somehow, in her head, my crimes had affected her whole family. Jewelers had their insurance money. She wasn't an owner but a clerk. What the hell was she talking about?

I stood for sentencing. Before the judge decided, he asked me a few more questions. I responded like little Doris Payne who needed to find a way out of some shit.

"Do you have remorse for what you have done?"

"Sir, I'm not sure what things you are referring to that I've done wrong."

He talked to my attorney as well in trying to figure out what he was going to do. He seemed exhausted, like he just wanted to go home and be done with it all. He said because I'd made a career out of stealing and wasn't going to stop, that I had to be put away.

I wanted to tell him that white men never did their time for stealing me and my people. I wanted to take him back to the scene of the crime: milking diamonds out of the mother-land until she was pillaged and war-torn. But I heard Mom telling me that I didn't have to say everything that was in my head.

The judge sentenced me to five years in the Central California Women's Prison Facility at Chowchilla, without bail.

My attorney asked the judge to reconsider. She knew that would put me in a facility of violent offenders. Based on my health issues, she didn't think I would be able to survive a year let alone five years.

I felt like my soul was bleeding out through my feet. He glanced at me and looked down like he was ashamed of what he was about to do to his own mother. Then he struck his gavel and it was over.

CHAPTER 25

RECKONING

ONE DAY, I SAT IN THE VISITING ROOM AT Chowchilla with Ronny. "Just mind your business, Mom. Just mind your business." But my roommate was sitting there with her boyfriend, and I knew what he was doing. She had told me he was having her swallow bags of cocaine and then shit them out to sell. I wanted to signal her not to do it again.

Months earlier, the facility had decided it was going to integrate and mix the cellblocks. No more separating the whites, Blacks, Asians, and Mexicans. It was a dumb idea, but I didn't really give a fuck. I was still numb. They came and asked me, like I had a choice, "Miss Payne, do you mind if we put Rochelle in here?"

I looked out from my bottom bunk, where I lay with my arm on my forehead to hold me in place. She was missing two teeth and had greasy black hair. I might be in for a heap of redneck trouble, but I knew not to show it. "I don't care who you put in here."

The first thing she said to me was "Are you scared of me?"

I told her I'd grown up in a coal-mining town with white people like her. "My mom used to put me in the porch swing and go to the store. She would tell me not to move till she got back because if I did, the white people would steal me and eat me." I made that shit up, but I liked how she stood there feeling the space in her mouth with her tongue, thinking about it.

She reminded me of Norma, who had worked at Euclid Manor with me. After a while, we became close. I was like her mother. I had told her to quit selling shit for that guy.

Ronny sounded like my mother. "Mind your business, Mama, and you won't get mixed up in other people's stuff."

I kept my eye on Rochelle. *Fuck!* Sure enough, she let her hair hang down in her face and pretended like she was eating the bag of chips her boyfriend had gotten her from the vending machine. Down went one small bag with a gulp of Sprite. Down went another. *Damn, damn.* I could have told her—water, not anything with acid. I knew that shit back from the days of scraping bags and knowing how the drugs came in and went out. She fell backward off the bench, went into convulsions. She died right there.

They cleared the visiting room and put us on lockdown.

ONCE THEY HAD integrated things, the brutality from the Black female inmates was equal to the brutality of the streets. Sometimes they would kill a woman. I saw them take out the dead bodies. I wished I was healthy and young enough to do something.

I avoided it because of my age. I don't think they wanted to hit someone who looked like their mother, but I was still scared to death in there. It was the worst for the Asian women with the fear and no control, because the Black women thought they were docile. I had seen men beat on women. But in prison, women were locked in a cell with their abusers. And I was locked up with the sound.

My first night, thudding noises came through the cinder blocks. The other inmates had learned to sleep through them, the way I had learned to sleep with the sound of traffic outside our house on Hough Avenue in Cleveland. But I never got used to the sound of Mom's body slamming against the floor in her and Daddy's bedroom, Mom's grunts when he hit her in the gut. The walls of a Slab Fork, West Virginia, clapboard house could only hold so much.

The cinder blocks couldn't hold the sounds either. Brenda, a big six-foot Black woman, had a face that reminded me of the knots in a tree in the backyard when I was a kid. Her fists were the size of big rocks. Her cellmate was an Asian woman who had killed her husband for beating her. This was a cruel way for her to live out her punishment, a purgatory of daily beatings from this mean Black devil of a bitch.

My cellmate took deep breaths in her sleep and exhaled in long snores between the sounds of *whoom*, *whoom*, and the woman hollering. I ran to our door and yelled, "Guard! Guard!" But it was like expecting one of my brothers to wake up and get Daddy off Mom.

She just sat there on her stool and raised her stick at me.

That Asian woman let out one last *humph* of air, and I surrendered myself to the floor in tears. There wasn't anything to do but wait till morning to see if she was alive.

I didn't know how brutal my mother had had it till I dealt with that. Every night I thought that woman would die, but she would just have one eye swollen shut or a knot on her head. She wouldn't hold her head up when we were marched to the showers or to the yard.

Sweet Jesus! I prayed every night, "I swear I won't steal nothing else, Baby Jesus. Just let me out of here."

My new cellmate was a skinny Black girl from Missouri who, from the rings around her eyes, looked like she had been on crack or something. She didn't mind me calling her "Crack," thought that shit was funny. She told me that everybody needed a project in their head to get through their time. She promised she was gonna open one of those stores where people come and paint ceramics. I told her, "That's the dumbest damn thing I ever heard of." We laughed good.

She said, "What you got better than mine, Granny?"

"Chile, I'm going down south to write my book."

She about fell out her bunk laughing. "Every nigga in here gonna write her prison memoir. You got to do better than that, Granny."

We played the dozens like that about our projects, and

it helped to keep me distracted. I sat in the mess hall and pretended to paint.

She said, "What the hell you doin', Granny?"

"Painting my little ceramic pig." I cracked up.

She pondered over some invisible thing on the table, then flipped her hand over once and looked closer.

"What you doin', Crack?"

"Reading Granny's prison memoir."

IT WAS COMING up on spring. I had been there more than a year, scared to death every night. Now on the other side of the cell there was another Black woman with a white prison wife. Through the vibration of the wall I could hear the white woman grunt from the pain that cut off her windpipe each time she was stomped. The guard wouldn't unlock the door no matter how many times I told them to come. I would hum to myself with toilet paper in my ears until I fell asleep. Still, I would wake up yelling, "Mom!"

At some point I got to looking at every obscure corner in that cellblock, focused on finding a place to die.

One morning, before chow, a female guard came and rattled me out of my bunk. "Granny, come on. Let's go."

I had served eighteen months. In those eighteen months, I had been in the infirmary six times for intestinal pain. I thought I was dreaming. I was back in the Greyhound bathroom all curled up in the tub. I just lay there looking at her, waiting for the next thing to happen in the dream.

"Let's go, Granny! Up!"

They weighed me. I was eighty pounds half naked. That meant I could get out of there. I had lost a lot of my body weight. I stood on the scale and said out loud, "Thank you, Baby Jesus! I swear I ain't stealing shit else."

I can't speak for God—no one can speak for God—but I figured he had given me my lickings for what he felt like I had done wrong, and that was all right with me. I felt new and knew what to do.

When I got back to Cleveland, there wasn't much to live on after Mr. Morrie Nidus's bank took advantage of my jail time and foreclosed on the house in Shaker Heights. I hocked all but my most precious things, and that was just enough to put down a few months' rent on a penthouse in Atlanta and get myself to the chocolate city.

My second weekend in town, I went into a mall to pick up a few things. I remember having to stop because it seemed like the floor was tilting. Then I saw little specks like bubbles in a soda bottle, and I woke up in the hospital.

The doctor said they had to run a battery of tests to see if I had stomach cancer, but the biggest problem was an intestinal infection. Rhonda came down a couple of weekends but had her own work, and I was too proud to ask her to just come and stay. I was too proud to tell her I didn't know how I was gonna pay the hospital bill. I was in and out of it for days on painkillers.

I thought I was dreaming this shit until I got better, but one of the Black nurses was so sweet to me and made it like I was hers. She told the other nurses, "Don't give her this.

Be sure to give her that." She would be all sweet on me. "How are you today, Mama?"

It felt good to have somebody taking care of me without me having to ask or burden anybody. After a few weeks, she got to talking like, "Somebody has had a hard time in the world, yeah?"

I told her a few things, because I swear I thought I was about to die, so I figured why not let somebody know about my shit. She heard it all: Mr. Benjamin, Babe, Cartier, Van Cleef & Arpels, the FBI. Next thing I know, this young lady was acting like my self-appointed caretaker. "You come home and stay with me when you get released so somebody can take care of you, Mama."

Before I got released, she had some folks she said were producers come to my bedside. This Black man and woman were large folks, like the elders at Robert's church. They had me sign some papers for my story. The young lady said, "These are good people, Mama. They'll help you tell your story."

I put my signature down.

I swear before God in heaven there ain't nothin' like healing up after a long convalescence and realizing that you don't want nothin' except to get your life back. This young woman's house was cluttered with fake wooden African artifacts and statues, all kinds of prints and woven tapestries, and smelled like one too many tree oils. I felt like a prisoner with her coming home and being like "Mama this" and "Mama that." She didn't even have a landline telephone, and where were the movie people who were supposed to be telling my story?

One morning I got myself dressed and walked to the McDonald's and begged to use their phone. I sat in the manager's office and called my son, Ronny, then called Attorney Berk. They both said the same thing to me. Leave that woman's house and find out what you signed in the hospital.

When you're hungry and sick, time does a strange thing. You remember all mornings as the same morning, and sleep connects all the nights in a way that feels endless. I walked into Walmart—maybe it was the same day. I had my prescription crumpled in my pocket and handed it to the pharmacist and didn't stand in the line waiting for them to get it ready. I acted like I was at Harper's Market and went and got me some groceries in a little basket. Milk, bread, a bag of apples, some potatoes, onions, carrots, and a meaty steak. I came back, got my prescription, and hesitated for a minute before walking out the door. I said thank you to the greeter on my way out and rolled toward the sliding doors with the beeping noise trailing behind me.

I was sitting in the back of a cab while the driver put the unbagged groceries in the trunk when three security guards came out and asked him to stop what he was doing. They tapped on the glass and said to me, "Ma'am, just stay in the car."

When the police arrived, the store manager let me keep some of the groceries, but I went to the precinct for fingerprinting. They didn't want me in a cell. So I was kept in some conference room, and officers walked by saying, "There she is," and talking about "The news stations aren't gonna leave until they get to talk to her."

I stood before a judge the next day. He didn't seem like he wanted to be bothered with the cameras in his courtroom. He let me go on house arrest with an ankle monitor.

Attorney Berk called to let me know that the contract for my story was not enforceable because it had been signed under duress and when I was not of sound body.

I don't know if I ever sat still, waiting for things and people to move into place so I could have what I wanted, but age can make a woman sit her ass down and quit "doing" in order to get. I stayed in the comfort of my penthouse for days that all ran into each other. Ensure for breakfast, CNN and the news of Trump, afternoon conversations with the man who came and got my trash and brought me my smokes, sunset on the balcony, and dinner from the little box of groceries my daughter had delivered to my door. Then the day ended and started again.

DVVS

A diamond with a D color grading is the brightest of all the grades—colorless. A diamond with a clarity rating of VVS is a gemstone with no noticeable internal inclusions or surface blemishes that can be seen without magnification. While a stone with a DVVS rating is not without its flaws, it is, however, a stone of extraordinary quality—with light-catching brilliance and envy-inducing fire. No matter how you cut it, a DVVS is a diamond to be admired.

(*D* is also for Dink and Doris.)

STAND ON MY BALCONY IN MY HOME IN ATLANTA. I cry, satisfied, because I can. And I thank Baby Jesus. I light up a big-ass joint. My bony cheeks suck in the satisfying burn of the smoke. The butt end glows the same color as the orange sunset over the skyscrapers in Atlanta, Paris, London, Tokyo. I wrap my pin-striped mohair coat around my shoulders and head to dinner.

I am in my eighties, with my press and curl on my silver crown.

So now you know the *true* story of Doris Payne.

Did I imagine some of this, make it up, elaborate it, polish it like a good diamond, make you want to look at it—make you smile?

You have to decide.

And you have to tell people what they want to hear. You have to let people see what they want to believe. You have to believe it first.

ACKNOWLEDGMENTS

I would like to thank Attorney Blair Berk—it was she who believed in me unconditionally. She allowed me to talk and say everything that was in my soul. I want to thank Baby Jesus. I want to thank my agent, Scott Mendel, who is a genius and made me feel proud and thought my story was worth something. Thank you to my editor, Tracy Sherrod. Working with her is how it should be. I appreciate my co-writer, Zelda Lockhart, who did some good listening, could see my life, and helped me to think about, remember, and feel people in my life, especially my mom. Thank you to Maya Corneille for her careful read of the manuscript, and to gemologist Nellie Barnett for bringing forth some important details about diamonds. Thank you to the editorial team at HarperCollins and Amistad, especially Judith Curr and John Jusino.

ABOUT THE AUTHOR

DORIS PAYNE was born in Slab Fork, West Virginia. She is the daughter of a coal miner and the second youngest of six siblings. Her career as an international jewel thief spans six decades.